higher education / Howard L. Smith.

al change—United States.   I. Title.

ble.

81

Library of Congress Cataloging-in-Publication Data

Smith, Howard L. (Howard Lee), 1949–
    Taking back the tower : simple solutions for saving
    p. cm.
    Includes bibliographical references and index.
    ISBN 978-0-313-36274-3 (alk. paper)
    1. Education, Higher—United States.   2. Education
LA227.4.S582 2009
378.73—dc22   2008047795

British Library Cataloguing in Publication Data is avail

Copyright © 2009 by Howard L. Smith

Library of Congress Catalog Card Number: 2008047795
ISBN: 978-0-313-36274-3

First published in 2009

Praeger Publishers, 88 Post Road West, Westport, CT 068
An imprint of Greenwood Publishing Group, Inc.
www.praeger.com

Printed in the United States of America

The paper used in this book complies with the
Permanent Paper Standard issued by the National
Information Standards Organization (Z39.48-1984).

10   9   8   7   6   5   4   3   2   1

CONTENTS

Acknowledgments

Occasionally in life a person comes along who epitomizes the best of the very best in a field. With respect to enlightened academic leadership that person is Dr. Bob Kustra, president of Boise State University. His visionary and energetic guidance has truly inspired students, faculty, staff, alumni, and the greater Boise/Idaho community. I too have benefitted immensely from his leadership and accordingly dedicate this book to him.

The views expressed in this book are solely the author's and do not necessarily reflect the opinions or policies of academic institutions with which he is or has been affiliated.

Chapter 1

PRELUDE TO CONSTRUCTIVE EVOLUTION

Taxpayers are sounding a clarion call about problems besetting higher education. Especially alarming is the persistently rising cost of a four-year undergraduate degree, a trend that has sent admissions and enrollments plummeting in even the hottest fields. Nationwide, the largest number of degrees has been conferred in business. Yet, over a seven year period, *Business Week*'s Top 30 MBA programs experienced a 30 percent decline in applications; in some cases the rate exceeded 50 percent (Merritt, 2005). Sky-high tuition is the apparent culprit, but college deans and university admissions officers acknowledge lingering difficulties foreign students face in obtaining visas to study in the United States as well as diminishing long-term economic returns students reap from educational investments.

Declining admissions may be exacerbated by a soft economy. For example, recession-driven, state-mandated enrollment caps for Florida's state university system have forced many institutions (e.g., Florida State University, Florida Gulf Coast University, University of South Florida, and University of Florida) to become more selective in student admissions—fewer seats are available (Braun, 2008). This pressure is spreading nationwide as states try to grapple with ever-tightening budgets. Even if our economy regains its vitality, The *New York Times* reports that the number of high school graduates will peak over the next two years, resulting in fewer college applications for the long run (Lamb, 2008).

If a perfect storm were to occur, admissions could be severely hurt by fewer seats available (due to budget constraints), fewer applicants (due to demographics), and rising tuition costs. This is a sea change that higher education must carefully monitor because crucial variables that might precipitate disaster are lining up.

Former Harvard president Derek Bok (2004) claims that universities are shortchanging their fundamental educational missions in an effort to stay financially afloat. Commercialization is rampant across virtually all areas of university endeavor—athletics, research, continuing education, alumni relations, and fundraising. Bok observes that practically everything is up for sale, and he prescribes broad policy changes to remedy these trends. Bok's concerns are not new; they have been echoed by other academic authorities in the past (Altbach, 1998; Gould, 2003; Kerr, 2001; Slaughter, 1999).

Universities are fighting for much more than financial survivability; they are also striving to maintain academic integrity (Bok, 2006). Substantial criticism has been directed toward universities regarding unprofessional faculty conduct and deterioration of academic culture. Sensational accounts of faculty members' irresponsible behaviors make entertaining reading (Sykes, 1989; Professor X, 1974). But even sober and balanced treatments suggest that an underlying malaise runs very deep (Sowell, 2003; Kimball, 1998).

Universities continue to be raked over the proverbial coals for their ineptitude and callousness toward intelligent stewardship of entrusted resources (Fish, 2008). Both positive and negative consequences accompany this scrutiny. On the one hand, continuing criticism motivates universities to take a harder look at what they are doing and to weigh outcomes from delivering higher education. On the other hand, few practical suggestions seem to surface (from those being critical) that move higher education beyond the status quo. It's easy to criticize but much more difficult to posit solutions with a decent chance of being implemented.

This propensity to criticize without suggesting tenable practical solutions is not very different from an insightful experience that occurred during my graduate studies. I had the good fortune of participating in an interdisciplinary program devoted to comprehensive health services planning. Classes in public health and medicine waxed eloquently about the sad state of affairs in health care. Seminar discussions had us spending hours lamenting the health system's failure to function efficiently as a system should. For course assignments we ferreted out duplication, waste, and haphazard policies that increased the price tag of delivering patient care services while contributing to errors that often cost people their lives. In case analyses we probed the unholy trinity of hospital-physician-administrator relations and how that wobbly three-legged stool could be counted on to collapse beneath patients. We became experts at denigrating healthcare providers and health services. That was on Monday and Wednesday.

Fortunately classes were also offered on other days. Every Tuesday and Thursday I would assiduously trundle across to the other side of campus for a breath of fresh air at the business school. After depressingly dark discussions of problems continuing to strangle health care on Mondays and Wednesdays, business classes were full of optimism and action. Instead of being hopelessly mired in the muck of what was perceived to be intransigently insolvable healthcare delivery constraints, the b-school professors espoused hope. Their message was in distinct juxtaposition with the health delivery side. My colleagues and I left classes with the sense that no thorny problem or depressing dilemma was too difficult to overcome. Even enormously complex issues were potentially solvable. What a refreshing change this attitude was—akin to receiving a "get-out-of-jail-free" card in Monopoly.

We were introduced to exciting methodologies for solving problems and making decisions. Intricate quantitative techniques such as linear programming became more than mere mathematical exercises in crunching numbers. Business professors showed us how these analytical models could be used conceptually in framing problems, objectives, constraints, and pathways to an optimum solution. Most of these tools were algorithms that needed to be deployed in the correct context. A few classes touched areas of non-linear thinking and managing chaos. In every class, without exception, there was hardly a thought—nary a word—implying that a situation was despairingly beyond repair. We left with the attitude that a proper amount of analysis and a judicious application of appropriate technologies could lead to a brighter future.

Higher education needs less of the public health/medicine syndrome and more, much more, of a business philosophy. Instead of obsessing about what's wrong with universities, it's time to innovate and solve problems. But many academics are not very receptive to change. They would rather continue deploring the plight of higher education than actually do anything about it.

All of that said, it is very critical to acknowledge that universities aren't business enterprises. Nor do we want them to become perfect replicas of corporations competing in a free enterprise system. Such a proposition fails to understand the fine (and not so fine) nuances of higher education and corresponding highly redeeming traits that have made U.S. universities globally renowned as intellectual powerhouses. A blind transfer of business technology wouldn't make for good academics; it would unquestionably throw higher education into revolution.

Instead, there is a middle ground where the very best of business practices may be skillfully combined with plain old commonsense thinking. This formula should go a long way toward improving the paramount qualities of academic institutions while simultaneously rectifying the lingering glitches.

Unlike popular treatises that dwell on what's wrong with our universities and colleges, *Taking Back the Tower: Simple Solutions for Saving Higher Education* focuses on commonsense solutions—relatively simple ways of solving problems. As opposed to obsessively talking about issues in a closed loop, this book addresses solutions at a university level where a renaissance is very achievable. The entire system of higher education has proven too much to tackle at once, but constructive evolution can begin brick by brick, university by university, until our once-respected system is thriving once again.

Taking Back the Tower is a compendium of lessons learned after serving almost two decades as vice president, dean, and associate dean at various universities and after thirty-plus years as a tenure-track faculty member. When I began as a dean, the average life of an accredited business school dean was 3.5 years. The rapidity with which deans are turned into toast by business schools may explain why only one in five institutions attains accreditation. One academic wag compared being a business school dean to a fire hydrant and the faculty to a pack of dogs. This was an extraordinarily perceptive insight.

Almost twenty years of administrative service gave me virtually boundless opportunities to grow both personally and professionally. I found myself doing and accomplishing things that I never dreamed possible. At the same time I accumulated incredibly valuable insights about people—their behavior, thought processes, incentives, desires, strengths, and shortcomings. Some of the insights are not very flattering regarding human motivations and spirit, but others give cause for optimism to soar.

Many of the vignettes discussed in this book come directly from my own experience. However, a single individual's experience is not the sole source of data on which *Taking Back the Tower* is based. Over the years, I accumulated many penetrating insights, examples, and case experiences from colleagues in academic units within my institutions as well as from colleagues at other universities. Inevitably, presidents, provosts, deans, and department chairs share with one another as a means to gain perspective, to keep abreast of trends at comparable institutions and within the professional field at large, to validate interpretations, and to form judgments that may influence decisions.

Sitting on a council of associate deans, deans, or vice presidents; sharing luncheon musings with another dean or department chair; discussing an issue with a group of department chairs; bouncing an idea or preliminary decision off an associate provost; or seeking senior faculty counsel are only a few of the many effective ways to collect internal information and insights. I used all of these approaches, and many more, quite liberally.

Professional meetings and academic conferences have also been particularly fruitful as external sources of awareness, enlightenment, and understanding. Collegial sharing in these venues added abundantly to my experiential base. Administrators and faculty tend to be very candid when outside their local academic communities. They feel less threatened and vulnerable. Professional meetings cultivate an environment of anonymity. Tongues begin to wag as relative strangers try to one-up the other in terms of a story's incredulity. Even if I never said a word at an academic meeting and only listened (admittedly seemingly impossible for any academic), I would come away with an astounding wealth of information and insights.

Due to the sensitive nature of this book's content I have altered various facts such as names, titles, and affiliations of people and organizations to maintain confidentiality. Any resemblance to actual events, locales, or persons, living or dead, is entirely coincidental. Please remember that I have enjoyed long relationships with more than nine universities, so it would be erroneous to assume attribution of any example to a specific university. However, make no mistake about it: *All* of the examples cited are from actual experiences. As bizarre as they may seem, none of this book is fiction. My imagination is not fertile enough to artificially construct the weird turns of events, wacky behavior, peculiar thinking, and unimaginable theater presented in these pages. Even the best scriptwriter Hollywood has to offer couldn't possibly make this stuff up.

At the same time I believe it is essential to remember one of most important lessons I learned very early in academia: *There are (at least) two sides to every story.* Thus, for every wacko view or incident, there are offsetting or parallel storylines. Most often staff and faculty would rise far beyond an occasion and set my heart soaring about the possibilities of higher education. A little illustration serves as a case in point.

I once reported to a very astute provost who wanted to encourage faculty to greater achievements. Extremely low faculty salaries were a challenge confronting my college. As a result I approached the provost with a proposal to address at least a smidgen of this insidious market inequity. The provost agreed that if faculty could alter how they taught their classes to save resources, those resources would then be plowed back into faculty salaries. There are many creative ways for achieving this goal; we would leave it up to the faculty to decide what approach they wished to implement.

Each department adopted a slightly different plan, but most relied on permanent faculty teaching larger classes to reduce the number of part-time adjuncts. The salary savings from using fewer adjuncts were reinvested in full-time faculty members' salaries.

One department balked.

Senior faculty in that department decided that they did not want to increase their salaries at the expense of larger class size. They felt that larger class size would do a disservice to student education. They were unwilling to sacrifice pedagogy for a bit more take-home pay. That's a pretty impressive response from folks whose salaries were well below national levels. So, please keep this lesson in mind as we examine the dysfunctional side. The intent of *Taking Back the Tower* is to focus squarely on the non-performing side of academia to learn about strategies for resolving problems. However, even as we focus on the down side, we should continually remember that academia is blessed with many excellent faculty and staff possessing hearts of gold.

Some in the academic community will be uncomfortable with this book because it relies on qualitative, rather than quantitative, research methodology. They should remember the rich scholarly legacy from cultural anthropology and sociology that draws on field studies of personal insight, oral history, and storytelling.

Others may criticize the relative paucity of citations from prior literature. Please understand that in many respects the academic establishment has already demonstrated an inability to solve its major problems. For decades we have collected data, studied, discussed, and reported on the problems besetting universities. Some academicians—infamous and eminent—have pontificated about the problems and conjectured romantic solutions. Little of this has worked because what's needed is to reverse the academic algorithm of thinking.

I have eschewed academically safe approaches in *Taking Back the Tower* because universities and colleges can only be saved by a fundamentally different way of thinking and behaving. We need a radically transforming evolution not perpetuation of the species. Indeed, the higher education establishment is an important part of the very reason why problems persist instead of being resolved.

Consequently, I decided to cut out the chaff of endlessly boring documentation and exhaustive reference to academic experiments—formal and informal, successful and not—in other settings, other institutions. The intended audience of *Taking Back the Tower*— taxpayers, legislators, regents and trustees, faculty, academic administrators, and staff—isn't really interested in all that academic pomp and circumstance. They merely want to know how to fix the problems.

The very kernel of truth underlying *Taking Back the Tower*, the dirty little secret, is that lasting answers to problems in higher education are gracefully simple and founded on an old-fashioned good dose of common sense. Other fields of human endeavor, notably business and to an extent public policy and public management, have employed technologies that I advocate for academia with startling consistency and impressive results. Nonetheless, a few sectors in our economy, such as higher education and health care, have successfully maintained their status quo, fighting progressive change every inch of the way. Guess what? Sand in their hourglass of resistance is about to run out.

Higher education is literally ripe for a fundamental revolution. The public is tired of spending so much for so little. Citizens are wondering why they have to struggle with the outfall of a global economy while academicians remain almost immune. Taxpayers aren't going to put up with it much longer, nor should they. Not when there are very straightforward resolutions for the predicament facing academia; not when there are easy ways to instill some sanity.

The purpose of this book is to consider several elegant common-sense solutions for saving higher education. This agenda of corrective strategies is based on a fundamental philosophy of nonlinear thinking. It's time to think quite differently about the nature of the crisis and how simple solutions might be used to expeditiously rebuild world-class university education in this nation.

The term "elegant" has two meanings that are apropos to this application. In one sense, elegant implies a level of gracefulness. Lasting solutions must be widely embraced by diverse constituents of universities. Graceful solutions are those that attend, for the most part, to the needs, aspirations, and intellect of taxpayers, regents, higher education administrators, faculty, staff, and students. At the same time graceful solutions are also creative and to the point, the second implication of an elegant solution. They are very efficient in resolving issues without excess complexity.

Taking Back the Tower adopts a viewpoint that there is no one best way to achieve meaningful progress. One of the overwhelming issues before universities is the prevalence of such a large number of problems—funding, access, quality, productivity, outcomes assurance, and learning efficacy to name a few. No single agenda can possibly solve all the problems. But, we don't need 100 percent of the problems resolved to make dramatic improvements. As a result, this book adopts a Pareto approach by addressing 20 percent of the causal factors that generate 80 percent of the perturbations. If universities work only on this 20 percent, they will achieve startling gains and once again demonstrate the sort of leadership the public expects from intellectually gifted academics.

At points, this book is brutally honest and critical; it will make some uncomfortable. But let us not forget that through education is the promise of a better future for each individual, society, and the world as a whole. Academia has stimulated phenomenal progress in the sciences and medicine. It has advanced the fine arts and culture of our country. Universities have nurtured exciting new discoveries across the whole gamut of disciplines and ultimately enhanced vast dimensions of life. The intellectual vitality of our society hinges on higher education. Throughout the history of Western society education has differentiated the enlightened from the uncivilized. It's merely time to take back the ivory tower.

Chapter 2

ACADEMIA: THE LAST GREAT BASTION OF RESISTANCE TO CHANGE

L eaping across a two-inch-deep puddle of stagnant water greasy with a sparkling iridescent rainbow sheen, I sought higher ground and drier shoes while fighting an unanticipated deluge. Forecasters indicated a strong storm front would just touch our northern mountains, leaving the rest of the state blowing east with dreaded spring winds—the bane of high desert country. They were wrong—again. Normally we don't complain about receiving such largesse. Every drop of moisture is welcomed, a special treat that fills the senses to overflowing. But my schedule was jam-packed with meetings that would leave me coming and going throughout the day. The very last indignity I needed was a good dose of sloppy weather.

Treading with utmost care up crumbling concrete steps slick as a waterslide, I raced toward an overhanging balcony and blessed relief from the falling torrent. How fortunate this storm didn't occur three weeks ago, when ice lingered in the shadows of our building. A disaster waited for an unassuming victim to fall and break a leg, hip, or other appendage. Despite our pleas to maintenance about a potential catastrophe and looming litigation as a result, we were not a sufficient priority.

Too many maintenance staff had already been cut with the latest budget reductions—a false economy if the wrong student, staff, or faculty member went down hard. An abundance of starving lawyers (produced by the university's very own law school) waited off-campus, circling like buzzards and eager to go for a pound-plus of flesh. They knew the drill. The university didn't have adequate legal staffing or funding to fight even the most transparent nuisance lawsuit. A settlement would be reached well before a case ever entered the court, handsomely rewarding the attorney and leaving the client with enough change for a latté but little else.

I skidded to a stop on dry concrete and shook like a drenched cocker spaniel, flinging droplets that twinkled like diamonds in a fluorescent glow from overhead beacons. Suddenly the lights switched off. What the . . . ?

Oh yes, an obstreperous staff member didn't want to upset maintenance with any extraneous service request because they were so short-staffed. The fact that a few people like me arrived at 6:07 A.M. when darkness reigned didn't justify hassling maintenance to alter the timing of safety lights. Besides, the problem would just take care of itself in the fullness of time. Each day the sun was coming up earlier.

Fumbling with too many keys in the night-dark alcove to our building, I repeated a familiar mantra about rising above small things and smaller people. Patiently fingering all of my keys—several more than once—the correct key luckily slid into the stubborn lock, and I was home free. Safely ensconced within the ivory tower, my slick big-city shoes slipped a time or two on our shimmering tile floor, but I finally made it to my office and desk without further challenges. A phenomenal pile of pink phone messages was stacked in one heap and a disheveled mound of assorted mailings, memos, and letters claimed more than its fair share of territory.

I only had fifty minutes before racing off to the first of two breakfast meetings this morning. Swinging around, I entered top secret code into the computer, unlocking the venerable tool of my trade, and waited while the screen blinked to life. It was always there, waiting eagerly to dump a new load of work in my lap. I scanned fifty-three e-mails that had accumulated since yesterday. Results were predictable: forty-seven qualified as garbage or merely information; one was from a faculty member whining about a department chair; three were meeting announcements from my boss (albeit without any agendas attached); one was from a long-lost friend (Are you the Howard Smith who attended Grossmont High School?); and only one—yes, just one—was of any importance.

Swiveling back to the mound of material front and center on my worn desk, I searched for items deserving immediate attention. If nothing else, as dean I had honed my skill at throwing out pieces of paper. What would the paper companies and post office do without me? My office provided secure employment for so many entities charged with spreading such poppycock. Conference announcements, cross-campus communiqués, advertisements, periodic reports, and copies of internal memos swamped my desk until I swept it to the best file of all—that cylindrical can waiting like a patient dog at my side.

I was chucking the whole mess into the trash can when a handwritten note caught my eye. It was from a colleague with the upper corner dated "Monday PM." This was Tuesday morning, so she must have given it to my assistant when I was off campus at a business community meeting. The note read, "Please write a short (max 100 words) letter to support my applications (sic) for a externally funded stipend to attend a conference this summer and give to me (w/ your signature) before 5:00 p.m. on Tuesday."

"How nice," I thought. I'll just drop everything and dash off the requested letter.

I glanced nervously at the clock; in four minutes, I would have to be in my car and roaring down the road if I wanted to make that first breakfast. Let's see, when could I comply with this request? The second breakfast involved a request for private funding to support a new faculty member's research. Then I had a committee meeting that I would cut short to attend a local Chamber of Commerce luncheon. After that, I would meet with an associate vice president about funding more evening classes. That meeting would go until a meeting of the deans' council that normally lasts past 5:00 P.M. Then it would be trips to the cleaners and food store before going home for dinner. Luckily this was one of two nights that I could catch up on that report to the provost about needed resources.

What about my colleague who had so generously given me twenty-four hours to comply with her request? When would she be served? I pulled up Word (since she often ignored e-mail) and prepared a short note: "Thanks for the opportunity to write a letter of recommendation for your funding application. Right now I have five letters of recommendation ahead of your request waiting to be prepared. Today my platter is completely full. Why not draft a letter for my signature?" As I dashed out the door, I slipped the note in her mailbox and prepared to scurry to my car in the rainy deluge.

Fast-forward several hours. After my morning committee meeting was over, I had six minutes before running to the Chamber of Commerce luncheon. At my office, the associate dean was waiting to fill me in on a mini-crisis, a department chair "needed just five minutes of my time" (which normally translated into an hour meeting), and my assistant handed me a reply from the colleague who requested the letter of reference. The colleague had just made it to campus and was impatiently waiting for a reply. While the associate dean rambled on about petty political matters I scanned the note and told him, "I'm listening." Multitasking isn't an option in these jobs.

The colleague wrote, "I am so sorry that I am not enough of a priority for you to prepare a letter of recommendation as requested. Ralph [my predecessor] never was too busy to help me out." Ah, well—there you go. I admit he was a much better dean than I, and he truly loved the job. The associate dean continued babbling while I thought of brilliantly devious ways to bring old Ralph back for another tour of duty. That would work just perfectly for me. But I shouldn't be so cavalier about this matter. My offended colleague is a senior tenured professor with sufficient clout and inclination to call a vote of no confidence if I slip up just once—a dean only has one chance with many non-supporters. This would open the door for her to retaliate.

The department chair in question desperately needed handholding. He was walking a razor-thin line between leading and being led by his faculty. He continually sought my counsel and consolation. I feared that if I wasn't there to mentor him he would lose control of his department and it would swing like a pendulum toward the Dark Side. That would disrupt politics throughout the school. Although I am more than up to a serious political confrontation (I could, after all, still count, and my count revealed that I hold a majority of support—barely—in this hallowed school), I have found them to be a time, energy, and emotional drain. Well, the associate dean will have to provide succor until I have time to meet tomorrow. But would it be too late by then?

A day in the life of a dean—isn't it impressive? The preceding vignette is presented to provide modest insight into what goes on daily in the ivory tower. If you read carefully between the lines you will notice (at least) four significant points that might otherwise be overlooked in the detail:

1. Universities are fighting a serious problem relative to facility/building replacement and renewal. In many cases funds are available to construct new facilities but not to renovate existing buildings. This results in the deterioration of plant (such as concrete steps) and equipment to an extent that

safety is compromised and risk for litigation is dangerously high.

2. Faculty and staff members often possess the (bad) attitude that they are the customer rather than thinking that their customer is the university. This attitude undermines the ability of universities to effectively execute strategies and to reach intended goals.

3. Universities operate according to a bizarre Byzantine mix of collegial governance and consensus decision-making. Faculties essentially elect their leaders (i.e., department chairs and deans). This has serious implications for leader effectiveness.

4. Substantial time is invested by academic administrators, faculty, and staff during committee meetings designed to cogitate about operating practices and policy issues. No item is too insignificant to merit extensive discussion. Action can always be delayed in the interests of making certain everyone is on board.

These four issues might easily be overlooked in the vignette, but they are more than just trifling little superficial concerns. They imply that a once-mighty institution—higher education—is under siege.

What happens when an organization is unable to maintain its physical plant and equipment? In the corporate world, inability to renew building, plant, and equipment triggers a progressive downward spiral. As funds are pumped into operations, investments in maintaining and replacing physical assets atrophy. Corporations operating in monopoly positions can go for a long time under these constraints. But in a globally competitive world where technology spells the difference in making resources more productive, failure to renew, renovate, and replace physical assets is a sure recipe for disaster. And so it is with universities that are now facing the pressures businesses encountered years ago.

What happens when any organization fails to connect with customers or clients—when personnel see themselves as the foremost customer? Our world is filled with choices, and customers today don't hesitate to vote with their feet. Customers have a predilection for going where they are wanted, for taking their hard-earned resources and investing them in organizations that deliver the most value per dollar expenditure. Even public services, or so-called free goods, are held to higher expectations these days as customers—taxpayers—expect to receive service equivalent with their expenditures. And so it is with universities that are now facing a crisis in customer relations. Students, alumni, and taxpayers no longer tolerate self-centered faculty or staff. They expect to be treated in dignified, cordial, mature, and time-efficient (for the customer) ways.

How many occupations, or people, have a guarantee of lifelong employment? Criminals serving life sentences do. Universities that maintain tenure do. Beyond this, the number is fairly small. Any time society offers someone the prospect of lifelong employment, even long-term employment, there is almost always a corresponding incentive for the employee to minimize effort and results. And so it is with universities. When faculty members become tenured, we inadvertently encourage them to demonstrate all of the wrong behaviors and to develop impossibly bad habits. Tenure makes it especially difficult for academic leaders to lead. If you cannot be terminated, then you have the latitude of making it difficult to be led, if not outright refusing to be led. Universities vitally need a healthy dose of *followership* to empower academic leaders.

Corporations jealously guard the use of employee time. They know that every second is either a potentially productive second or a wasted second. Therefore, they seek to attain the highest and best use of time—of any resource for that matter. Corporations have lots of meetings; they are a necessary part of doing business. But high-performing corporations do not allow meetings for the sake of meeting. They are very careful about overdosing on meetings to the detriment of getting things done. Meetings must accomplish a specific end and follow a predetermined agenda, otherwise they are called off in high-performing firms. The opposite occurs in universities. Higher education luxuriates in the poor use of time. This reflects arrogance toward the goal of highest and best use of resources.

ELEGANT SOLUTIONS FOR SAVING ACADEMIA

A surprising axiom often disregarded by administrators and executives in higher education is that the problems confronting our colleges and universities are extremely easy to solve. Most educational situations call for commonsense approaches that have stood the test of time in public management, business, and high-performing third sector (nonprofit) organizations. Remedies suggested in the following pages are almost embarrassingly elementary. Successful organizations around the world use these ideas as normal operating policy in the daily course of delivering goods and services. They are so basic, so fundamental, that most high-performing organizations don't even give a second thought to them—other than making certain they are implemented with great effectiveness. And this level of comfort is precisely what higher education should strive to achieve regarding problem solutions and resource stewardship.

A visual rendering of *Taking Back the Tower* is presented in Figure 2.1. On the left-hand side, forces driving change create tumultuous pressures on universities to alter their status quo. This chapter (Chapter 2) addresses these forces that are endangering our institutions of higher education and their resistance to change. Indicators of the crisis are identified along with the leading rationales explaining why university leaders fail to change the existing state of affairs. They diligently perpetuate "situation-normal" within their institutions.

Chapters 3 through 8 speak to the right-hand side of Figure 2.1. Six commonsense solutions for saving higher education are proposed that together form an antidote for academia's resistance to change. Chapter 9 explores how these solutions can help take back the ivory tower and in the process kick out the barbarian element that hinders our beloved institutions from moving forward.

FORCES DRIVING CHANGE

Higher education has done an extremely good job of blindly ignoring realities that the rest of the nation and world have been grappling with the past ten years. In comparison, corporations have gone through several phases of reengineering (e.g., reduction in force, right-sizing, downsizing, and so forth) to meet foreign competition and global pressures. Now they face further rounds of redefinition and transformation. Nonprofit organizations and governmental agencies have also faced serious pressures to re-orchestrate how they deliver services.

Figure 2.1. Academia's Resistance to Change and a Common Sense Antidote

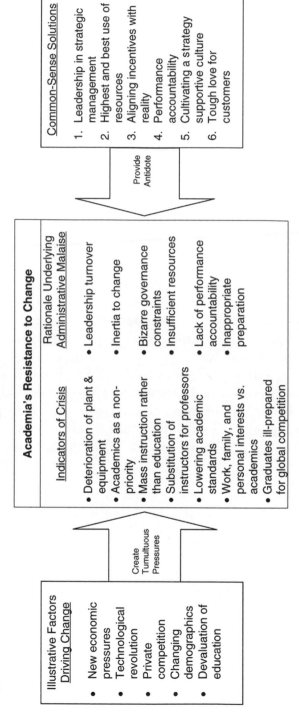

Academia's Resistance to Change

Illustrative Factors
Driving Change

- New economic pressures
- Technological revolution
- Private competition
- Changing demographics
- Devaluation of education

Create
Tumultuous
Pressures

Indicators of Crisis

- Deterioration of plant & equipment
- Academics as a non-priority
- Mass instruction rather than education
- Substitution of instructors for professors
- Lowering academic standards
- Work, family, and personal interests vs. academics
- Graduates ill-prepared for global competition

Rationale Underlying
Administrative Malaise

- Leadership turnover
- Inertia to change
- Bizarre governance constraints
- Insufficient resources
- Lack of performance accountability
- Inappropriate preparation

Provide
Antidote

Common-Sense Solutions

1. Leadership in strategic management
2. Highest and best use of resources
3. Aligning incentives with reality
4. Performance accountability
5. Cultivating a strategy supportive culture
6. Tough love for customers

Although citizens, government, and the private sector suffer from dramatic upheavals associated with the energy crisis, foreign competition, and domestic mishandling of the mortgage market, among many other factors, universities persist in behaving like it's "situation normal." They lumber along seemingly oblivious to pressures strangling the economic engine that enables many people to attend college.

As gasoline prices skyrocket, real estate values crumble, and the dollar plummets in value, prospects for many to attend college, even to complete their degree programs, have become very shaky. When the general populace spends less for goods and services, they inadvertently undermine economic support for students, especially those employed in the service sector. Eventually, demand for a college degree is tested in the marketplace of choices. Facing lower incomes and higher tuition costs, some students opt out of degree programs. As economic conditions worsen, a college degree becomes discretionary rather than obligatory.

Universities have traditionally seen demand for degrees rise in periods of economic hardship as people return to campus to pick up marketable skills. This premise may not hold true when the price of education combines with two drivers: lower short-term earning potential and higher long-run college loan debt. Universities persist in strolling down a garden path wearing rose-colored glasses that belie their crumbling fiscal foundations.

New Economic Pressures

Corporations have redefined themselves to thrive under new economic premises. Megacorporations are now leaner, flatter, less diversified, and more agile. They have to be if they want to compete and survive over the long run. And it isn't just the largest multinational or globally based corporations that have gone through the wringer. Even small local businesses face globally competitive forces that are passed down the food chain. Many small businesses have been caught off-guard as long-term customers have drifted away, lured by cost savings or higher quality products from firms they never dreamed of doing business with.

Even today, universities enjoy sufficient largesse to callously turn a deaf ear to the struggles others face. However, the economic revolution is rapidly catching up with higher education. Instability in the global energy market coupled with shaky worldwide financial institutions have increased economic vulnerability by an impressive order of magnitude. Public universities are watching state budgets shrink (rapidly in an increasing number of cases) and concomitantly more parties clamoring for their righteous piece of the public pie.

Throughout the United States, egregious fluctuations in the stock market associated with the home mortgage calamity, the energy crisis, leftover problems from the dot.com fiasco, and a lingering lack of confidence due to terrorism have hit private universities and public institutions hard in endowed funding. Public institutions generally experience less impact because their endowments often represent a smaller percentage of their revenue stream. Those relying on endowed investments for operating income have faced deficits of momentous proportions. These deficits are immediate and significant as far as implications for maintaining top-flight academic programs are concerned.

In many respects, public and private universities that have undergone budget cutbacks due to lower earnings potential on endowed funds have only experienced a small taste of what many corporations endured due to stiffer competition. Nonetheless, the impact is very real and significant in affecting not only current programmatic services but program building for the future as well.

Particularly hard hit are faculty and staff positions. Universities leave these positions vacant as a cash float while remaining faculty and staff are asked to do more; that is, increase productivity without commensurate changes in pay. Physical assets such as plant and equipment receive less maintenance or renovation, thus beginning the slippery slope of deteriorating buildings and landscaping. Technology acquisitions are delayed. Operating system improvements are put off. In short, universities know the sting of a skimpy pocketbook that businesses have faced for many years, albeit for slightly different causal factors and trends.

Technological Revolution

Technological advances have hit higher education in a multitude of ways at a time when funds are not readily available to support major equipment and software investments. Every university knows the perils of not remaining current with technology.

Research suffers because graduates are ill-prepared for the marketplace and not conversant in their respective fields. Thus, institutions of higher education face a desperate predicament. They cannot afford to be left behind in the currency of technological assets, but there are no promising revenue streams to fund technology acquisition.

As dean, I once sat through a presentation on a new student-centered software system that would totally revamp our student records. The academic administrator for this project (who was given a very fancy title) and his executive director made a "nice" presentation to my colleagues explaining how this software would really put some bells and whistles on our student records. Their presentation was cordial and warm. Who could argue with their admonition that we just had to purchase the system?

Well, I did.

After their presentation I asked how much this would cost and where funding would come from. Of course, this was excessively bad form. The chief academic administrator at the meeting answered this way: "We have no choice. This is a hugely important need, and we just have to move forward with it regardless of the cost. The price tag may be anywhere from $50 to 70 million. I don't know where the funding will come from, but we have no choice." I glanced down at the end of the table to watch another dean silently mouth: "We'll pay for it out of our budgets." He was right on target. How many other universities are plunging straight ahead with similar purchases or vitally needed equipment and software acquisitions they can ill afford?

In addition to raising the investments universities make in equipment and software infrastructure, technology is impacting the delivery of higher education. Many universities are experimenting and/or plunging straight ahead with electronic delivery. On the one hand, interactive televised delivery, classes over the Internet, and other electronic modalities have been acclaimed as the next frontier for university market penetration. On the other hand, it appears that fewer students (than originally projected) prefer to learn through electronic media. Universities have also encountered very high delivery costs in these programs, thereby threatening their aspirations to maintain quality approximating that of on-campus courses.

In some respects, technology is causing more problems than solutions in the classroom. Universities are grappling with

Web-induced plagiarism, text-message cheating, and term-paper purchasing. The phenomenal potential of electronic technology to buttress traditional education has also brought significant ethical problems into the classroom. Clever students are using digital pagers and cell phones to beat the system during midterms and final exams. Almost as quickly as new personal communications technology appears, inevitably some students figure out how to use the electronic assists in an unethical fashion.

Private Competition

Free enterprise is another prominent force driving change in higher education. Private universities have made considerable progress in what some term the "McDonaldizing" of education (Hayes and Wynyard, 2006). The most unscrupulous private degree mills sell education at a very high cost to a willing market of students, a sizeable percentage of whom (a) cannot meet higher academic standards associated with traditional university programs, (b) are basically interested in receiving a degree rather than an education, or (c) don't want to invest sufficient effort required for a degree with substance. These programs feed off a segment of the population that falls prey to repeated messages about conveniently earning a college degree—the message is almost never about learning or education.

It's hard to criticize individuals who fall for the romance of a quick degree (often through courses requiring less than half of the contact hours mandated by traditional universities) with limited studying and academic credit for life experiences. Why should these prospective students make it hard on themselves? These folks aspire ambitiously to get ahead in this world at the least possible inconvenience. Who can blame them? It's an alluring message made all that more credible by the failure of corporations to distinguish between traditional and entrepreneurial universities. Major corporations such as Intel, PeopleSoft, or AT&T have in the past been willing to pay all or part of their employees' tuition when they attend, for example, the University of Phoenix.

The bottom line for traditional universities facing private competition is that potential students are lost—students that represent important revenue in a budget-constrained world. This has led many universities to adopt slick customer relations programs (also known as enrollment management initiatives). Borrowing commercial technologies, universities nationwide are marketing to students in unprecedented ways to entice them to join their programs—to essentially spend tuition dollars on their campuses. Faculty members in particular resent this sort of corporatization of academia and the potential for traditional universities to inadvertently travel that slippery slope to selling degrees.

Changing Demographics

Changing demographics and attitudes toward higher education are adversely affecting the long-established planning premises of universities. Traditional college students once included those in their late teens and early twenties. They attended classes full-time and often lived on campus. Today, these same students are increasingly categorized as non-traditional students.

Students are less likely to complete their bachelor's degrees in four years. In fact the National Center for Education Statistics (2003) indicates that in the 1999–2000 academic year, the average time to degree completion for those students who did not interrupt their course of study was fifty-five months. Work is a major factor explaining why degree completion has been extended. Students who are employed as a means to meet college expenses work on average twenty-six hours per week. Half of these students indicate that this negatively impacts their class schedule and number of classes taken (National Center for Education Statistics, 2002).

The implications of these trends are quite robust. Universities have found that they must use new planning assumptions about demand for on-campus housing and the type/design of housing that is marketable. Course scheduling was formerly based on a cohort progressively completing classes from one semester to the next. Now students wander through curricula without following lock-step patterns. Student populations are also aging, which presents an entirely different set of expectations regarding instructional format and class accessibility. These and many other changes in student populations suggest greater difficulty for universities in planning operations and maintaining productivity across their asset base.

Devaluation of Education

Finally, Figure 2.1 suggests that education has become devalued at a time of inflationary costs and decreasing revenue streams. Universities are experiencing trouble in passing these costs to consumers because of the perceived decline in the value of education. Students view a direct correlation between earning a degree and landing a job. The value associated with earning a college education and pursuit of lifelong learning has depreciated. Students perceive a diminishing link between education and a career; a college degree has been rendered an entryway to a job, not a career.

As state and federal funding drops off, universities have an option of charging more in tuition to cover escalating costs associated with providing education. This strategy is flawed if customers do not perceive enhanced value from earning a degree. Customers only see high annual tuition increases that may not be covered by commensurate rises in subsequent earnings on the job. Their risk is that current education expenditures will not be offset by higher earnings potential. As a result, inflationary price increases dampen demand.

In sum, Figure 2.1 illustrates only *some* of the more important forces driving change in higher education. These forces create tumultuous pressures for institutions of higher education, stresses that universities have limited experience and capacity to manage.

INDICATORS OF CRISIS

I was visiting a state university in California and my hosts were pointing with pride to a new humanities building that was just being erected. It was an impressive structure, several stories tall, with a very appealing design. A big celebration was planned to inaugurate this hallowed addition to the university community—a work that was over ten years in the making. No doubt this building was something taxpayers, faculty, and students would point to with justifiable pride. It might also rectify this university's tendency to lose top quartile students to other institutions.

As we strolled around the perimeter my hosts pointed out the finer details. A student study lounge had an impressive view of the setting sun. Faculty offices were located away from classrooms cloistered on the first and second floors. Finer details were emphasized as my hosts gazed with appreciation, but my mind and sight were elsewhere. I could not help noticing that this beautiful building, so tastefully rendered by an architect with noble vision and lovingly constructed by a contractor sensitive to the architect's grand design, was surrounded by a virtual campus ghetto.

Deterioration of Plant and Equipment

Every campus building surrounding this new masterpiece, every single one, looked like it had been transported to campus from this city's low-rent district. They were appallingly shabby. Out of courtesy for my hosts, I didn't mention this dichotomy, but the spectacle was there for all to see. I was witnessing one of the tangible physical reminders of how bad things have become on university campuses, especially public universities. Buildings and equipment are not being renovated or replaced according to any intelligent master plan. It isn't that a plan is lacking, it's that funds simply are not available to maintain and repair physical assets.

Some might ask rather cynically, "What's the big deal? It's just a short-run phenomenon. When the cycle turns and universities are awash in funds, they can catch up." Right? Wrong!

First, we're just kidding ourselves if we think that such a turn of events is going to occur any time in the near future. Universities are having trouble funding operations, much less taking care of plant and equipment. Second, the image that a campus conveys is highly significant in how students view the quality of education they are receiving and how they view themselves. Disregard for physical surroundings easily translates into disregard for students and the implication that everything—especially the education—is second rate. That's not the message we want to be sending to our students.

My hosts continued the campus tour with a visit to the athletic facilities. No wonder this university had fielded a bowl team at least every other year for the past decade. No wonder the basketball team routinely made it to the NCAA tournament. The athletic facilities were luxurious, and athletes apparently were lavished with the attention and equipment to take their game to a nationally competitive level. It was impressive stuff.

Academics as a Non-Priority

Unfortunately this juxtaposition of athletics and academics embodies one of the indicators that something is seriously wrong on university campuses. As I took in the splendors of the athletic complex I had to check myself from blurting out the obvious—athletics were a higher priority than academics on this campus. That was nothing new. I was fully aware that the athletic facilities came out of a different budget and were generously supplemented by revenues generated by the athletic department. But something lingered in my craw about the disparity—the realization that alumni who provided so much of the funding for athletics took no pride in the academic side.

Our tour ended over at the student union building, a multipurpose structure offering study sites, food services, personal services, and entertainment. I wanted to warm up with a cup of tea while avoiding the height of rush hour traffic. My hosts had other engagements they needed to keep, so I inexplicably found myself sharing a table in the busy cafeteria with two students while I cradled my tea and them, their lattés.

Admittedly this was only a convenience sample of two students in one of this nation's thousands of universities. My academic colleagues would blanch at the inference that our conversation could shed any insights on trends in higher education. But to be honest, these were the same old tunes I had heard from students over and over again during the last fifteen years. Their stories went something like the following.

Mass Instruction Rather than Education

Both were supposed to be in class at that very minute—one in a mathematics class and the other in music appreciation. However, they found each other's company far more intellectually stimulating then the mass lectures that were drolly unfolding to hundreds of other students. The classes were simply too large for meaningful interaction. The instructors either read notes or flashed one Power-Point slide after another on the screen. These presentations added little to what the text had conveyed. It was the equivalent of mass instruction, not education.

Substitution of Instructors for Professors

Neither of their instructors were tenured faculty. One had entered the university's doctoral program in mathematics after completing bachelor's and master's degrees in her distant homeland. The other had apparently never been given any instruction in teaching effectiveness. Even the associated student body's paid note taker was falling asleep. The learning environment was equivalent to downing a sleeping pill and then turning on a continuous stream of white noise with one exception. The hard plastic chairs provided sufficient discomfort to keep light sleepers from nodding off.

Lowering Academic Standards

These students seemed not the least bit concerned about passing their class. They confidently responded that all you had to do was read the text once; going back over the material several times only raised difficult questions that never surfaced on the exams. A burgeoning test bank was on reserve at the library, and, with luck, the lazy instructors would select test questions for which you had prepared. All testing was true/false and multiple choice. And one implied that his girlfriend had aced the course the year before and would sit in for him during the exam. No effort was made to control for this sort of deception.

How did these classes compare to others? The students admitted that they were a little more lax than some of their other classes. After all, you would generally have difficulty faking a physical substitution of your boyfriend or girlfriend, but that didn't mean friends of the same gender wouldn't help out when called on for assistance. Furthermore, they noted that this entire academic year they had not been required to submit anything in writing—it was just too onerous a burden for the instructors to grade.

How many of this university's distinguished senior faculty had they enjoyed taking a class from over their academic terms? These students didn't quite grasp my question, and I provided a bit of explanation about tenured faculty versus adjunct professors, graduate assistants, teaching assistants, and doctoral students. One of my newfound friends could only remember two professors who held doctorates, but she didn't know their tenure status. The other had not, to his knowledge, been assigned a tenured professor, nor did he want to be. He had heard plenty of stories about their oddball behaviors and predilection to assign writing assignments and oral presentations in class.

Work, Family, and Personal Interests Versus Academics

One of the students apologized because she had to leave for work. This was also a convenient segue for me to leave. But as she departed, I asked her if she attended college full- or part-time. "Oh," she replied, "I'm taking a full load this semester." "And how many hours a week do you work?" I questioned. "I've cut back to thirty-five hours since I want to raise my grade point average." "Ambitious schedule?" I suggested. "No, but I don't see as much of my little daughter as I want to." And with that she spun on her heels and raced toward her waiting paycheck.

I was shaken by the entire experience, but I too had to run to meet a business colleague. He graduated from an Ivy League school and made it big time in a high-tech company whose name is held in inestimably great repute. At a previously appointed steakhouse we huddled around mediocre gin and tonics, both of us seeking solace after a long, tiring day. I mentioned my campus visit and asked his insights about graduates from that august institution and his firm's hiring practices on campus.

Graduates Ill-Prepared for Global Competition

The news was not good. He had found this university's graduates to be modestly proficient in oral skills, horrendous in written skills, and barely passable in critical thinking skills. His harangue went on and on. It was too painful, so I ordered a second drink. He sighed and looked back fondly on his college days some twenty years past. "What went wrong?" he asked. "How have we coddled college students to the point that they are brain-dead when they graduate? Why are we pouring millions of dollars down the drain and then hiring foreign college graduates to fill the plum positions in our firm?" As I hid behind my third drink I could not fathom an acceptable answer to this easy question. Ah, here come our sizzling steaks to the rescue.

Go across town and you are likely to hear the same story—different campus, same story; same indicators, more or less. A day in the life of a college campus varies little except at truly distinctive bastions of higher learning. Market forces, state and federal funding, faculty impediments, staff unionizing, and many other factors indicate that higher education is in a crisis. Sadly, the more things change in academia, the more they stay the same. Our once-great universities have been driven by benign neglect to a pervasive mediocrity. University leaders have not only failed to change this equation, they have perpetuated the status quo.

RATIONALES FOR RESISTANCE TO CHANGE

Why do university leaders fail to change the status quo? Answers to this question are as numerous as excuses from a teenager regarding why he/she missed curfew by an hour and a half. Figure 2.1 suggests several leading rationales regarding why academia fights so hard to keep from changing.

Leadership Turnover

The terms of university presidents, provosts, and deans are appallingly short. Many explanations help understand this phenomenon, and none of them are entirely satisfactory. Things move at glacial speed in universities, whether it is curriculum change, development of learning assurance, or strategic planning. That's just the way it is—it's an institutional cultural characteristic. Thus, because many academic leaders are aspiring to move up in the hierarchy of university-dom, they are reticent to come in and make waves. Even if they wanted to make revolutionary changes, the entire system operates to essentially thwart alterations to the status quo.

Because academic administrators occupy their positions for such short periods of time, there is a low probability that they will actually observe meaningful progress toward reforms they wish to implement. It's akin to moving a car-sized rock by physical force. You can keep pushing and pushing and get nowhere. You can solicit other people to help out. But, in the end a car-sized piece of granite is not going to move very far by human effort alone. Meaningful movement requires planning and the cooperative intersection of people and machines. You don't simply go out and push on a car-sized boulder and observe much progress. The same holds true for change within universities.

The most astute academic administrators who excel in decisive decision-making and purposeful implementation of change rarely stick around long enough in academic settings to see the results of their efforts. These talented people are lured away by better positions. It's the other administrators that we have to watch out for; the ones who aren't decisive or effective in managing change—those who act more like bureaucrats than executives. They shun altering the status quo because of anticipated adverse reactions from students, faculty, staff, other academic administrators, and trustees when rocking the ivory tower.

Inertia to Change

University leaders are also very sensitive to the prevailing inertia that prevents change within higher education. An applicable and quaint phrase that faculty like to banter about is, "This too will pass." Remember, faculty members are tenured. They're not going anywhere, so they may listen attentively as new leaders emerge at their college in the provost's office or the presidency, but faculty are seasoned pros. They have watched administrations come and go. In the end, they go. So why think that actual change will occur?

In the final analysis, too many academic leaders may be looking out for number one. In most cases presidents, provosts, and deans do not want to make big waves that ruffle faculty feathers because they are planning on moving to better positions. You don't earn accolades by stirring the pot and disrupting everyone's life. An upward-bound president or provost only wants to make wavelets—baby waves of change with the appearance of a huge agenda—a reality that's actually quite modest and has everyone feeling good.

For those blokes who love where they live or because of family or other personal reasons choose to remain at a university for years, they typically do not have an incentive to make large-scale change. These leaders know that as soon as you launch a change agenda, the big push back begins and doesn't let up. Big disruptions only cause more headaches and too many forces are at play trying to protect the status quo. Students, faculty, and staff are running around posturing as though they agree with the change agenda, but in reality they simply want to maintain things the way they have been. This frenetic posturing with subtle underlying resistance is known as "dynamic conservatism" (Schon, 1973). Ironically, academics publicly, and often vociferously, advocate change while doing everything in their power to prevent it.

After academic leaders have been burned one or two times in their change initiatives, there is a natural tendency to pull back and become more hesitant about introducing sweeping reform. This is exactly what faculty, staff, and lower administrators want. An academic administrator's plate is full enough without looking for problems. Thus presidents, provosts, and deans settle into an administrative mindset of maintaining their academic unit. They recoil from leading (in the managerial or executive sense) and devolve into caretakers.

Bizarre Governance Constraints

As Figure 2.1 suggests, even if academic leaders wanted to introduce sweeping reform, higher education is set up to block such efforts. Convoluted governance associated with faculty perquisites cautions leaders from leading. How many other organizations maintain a policy of allowing subordinates to vote on their leaders? In academe, department chairs and deans are subject to approval by faculty votes. At any moment, faculty may express their displeasure through a vote of no confidence. The same holds true for provosts and presidents primarily through the faculty senate.

Few other organizations immediately assume that it will take upward of a year to identify their next key leader. When a president resigns the natural assumption is that another academic year will expire before a new president takes the helm. Obviously there are exceptions, but it is more the rule that key leadership positions in academia are filled after a long, drawn-out vetting process. It is important to select the right woman or man for each position, but opportunity costs in drawn-out searches can be substantial.

Insufficient Resources

Resources affect the ability of academic leaders to perform their duties and as a result tend to reinforce the status quo. If a leader doesn't possess sufficient resources to effectuate change, she or he is going to think twice about stirring up trouble only to see an initiative fail. In a similar line of reasoning, presidents, provosts, and deans have overwhelming schedules. They do not have the time to shepherd key initiatives. Yet many also do not have sufficient high quality associate provosts or associate deans to ensure the effective execution of a change initiative.

Lack of Performance Accountability

Academic leaders resist change because their feet are not held sufficiently to the fire. Performance evaluation for presidents, provosts, and deans doesn't occur daily or weekly as in many high-powered and driven corporations. Annual reviews come only once a year and often as an afterthought. As a result, rigorous analysis and feedback tend to be lacking. The case of a promising young basketball coach who parlayed his rising star into several quick moves up the ladder illustrates this point. Athletic directors read his promise rather than his won/loss record. He is now coaching at a major university despite never having produced a winning season in his career.

Inappropriate Preparation

Finally, as Figure 2.1 indicates, university leaders resist implementing change because they have the wrong education, training, and experience. Most provosts and deans surface from the liberal arts or sciences. They have limited prior knowledge about management concepts and their applications, and they have been indoctrinated into protecting faculty perquisites. Above all, they just don't quite get the picture about fiscal matters and the relationship to operations management. They tend to think from a budget-plus-percentage-increase mentality when each year's budget rolls around.

Some universities have tried to circumvent this problem by seeking leadership talent from business, public service, or politics.

Notable leaders have surfaced because they brought with them crystal-clear objectivity and a willingness to do what is right rather than what's expedient to retain their jobs. However, the closer their position is to operationally managing faculty—such as at the dean level and lower—the less effective they become because they don't understand faculty cultures, and they do not possess academic credibility that inspires followership.

In sum, many rationales may be found regarding why academic leaders tend to resist instilling change in their organizations. These factors present a legitimate obstacle to reforming higher education. However, academic leaders' reluctance to do what is right as far as solving the problems confronting higher education effectively reduces them to benign bureaucrats. They perpetuate the crises and block reform they should be leading.

Common Sense As an Antidote

Despite academia's resistance to change, all is not lost. Common sense can prevail and serve as a powerful antidote that revitalizes higher education. The fundamental premise underlying *Taking Back the Tower* suggests that relatively simple, concise solutions can extricate universities from their malaise. We merely need to turn to the world outside the hallowed halls of universities to discover elegantly functional solutions to the problems besetting our college campuses.

Figure 2.1 outlines six commonsense solutions for introducing reform in higher education:

- Leadership in Strategic Management (Chapter 3)
- Highest and Best Use of Resources (Chapter 4)
- Aligning Incentives with Reality (Chapter 5)
- Performance Accountability (Chapter 6)
- Cultivating a Strategy Supportive Culture (Chapter 7)
- Tough Love for Customers (Chapter 8)

These chapters represent a foundation for changing much of what is wrong in higher education. But an agenda of strategies is only a list of aspirations unless it is effectively executed. Consequently, the final chapter (Chapter 9. Taking Back the Ivory Tower) addresses implementation of this agenda for change.

A Few Final Caveats

The primary focus of *Taking Back the Tower* centers on four-year colleges and universities that offer bachelor's degrees and graduate degrees and that may support a research mission. Community colleges—two-year colleges—typically possess a very specific teaching focus. Although many two-year colleges criticize tenure, some have followed four-year institutions in recognizing tenure or its equivalent. In recent years two-year colleges have progressively tried to mimic universities in the breadth of course and degree offerings. They have adopted the nomenclature of "university," implying that they want to run with the big dogs. Those that are following these trends can cite sound rationales for diversifying academic programs and mimicking faculty relations. Unfortunately they may be going down the same path toward mediocrity as their larger university brethren.

Public and private universities are treated as equals in *Taking Back the Tower*. Admittedly, private universities have much greater incentive to resolve their problems before they go belly-up. They generally do not enjoy that comfort of deep public pockets in times of financial exigency. Furthermore, many well-endowed private institutions have discovered how quickly their equity base can erode in a volatile market. Recent financial shortfalls have driven some private universities and colleges to full-on fiscal exigency. Thus, private universities may tend to be more receptive to the ideas suggested in this book and more progressive in adopting such reform as a matter of operating necessity.

Critics in the higher education establishment might find it preposterous that greater distinctions haven't been made in this book between two-year and four-year universities, between colleges and universities, between private and public universities, and between universities that pursue teaching missions versus those pursuing research missions versus those with blended research and teaching missions. Admittedly some very important distinctions exist among institutions in these categories, but when you get right down to it they are all organizations comprised of people—as students, faculty, staff, administration, and boards of directors or trustees—attempting to fulfill various educational missions. In the final analysis is there really that much difference among them?

What does matter is achieving reform in higher education to protect the long-run prospects of our educational institutions. Let the professional debaters pick nits about how public universities are so much different than private colleges or how research institutions should be exempt from prevailing market forces. While these dilettantes are carrying on their academic diatribes, the long-run prospects for their organizations will continue to erode. The goal they should be focusing on is the assurance of good stewardship of scarce resources—commonsense solutions for difficult resource problems—not academic debate that leads to further problems.

Chapter 3

LEADERSHIP IN STRATEGIC MANAGEMENT

Leadership in strategic management is absolutely critical for universities and higher education. Unless you know where it is that you want to go, any old path will take you to mediocrity. For decades, universities have cultivated lackadaisical attitudes about aspiring to do better. They are, after all, universities—institutions of higher learning where people earn degrees and receive an education. There's no rocket science about this, nor any reason to make university strategic planning any more complex than it really is. Right? Wrong. In truth, universities vitally need a clear sense of who they are, what they do best, and what direction they should pursue in the future. But this is only part of the strategic management challenge.

Simply utter the words "strategic planning" to a diverse group of students, staff and faculty members, alumni, community representatives, and administrators if you really want to see people yawn. How many times do they have to go through this exercise in futility? Big emotional discussions ensue, but complete agreement about a vision or mission is never reached. After hammering out a manifesto, the strategic plan just sits there. It's never used to make decisions or to guide resource allocations. It ends up becoming a bunch of platitudes resting comfortably on a bookshelf or languishing on a Web page. These thoughts cross their collective minds before they sprint to the door.

Stakeholders, the people who are affected by strategic plans and the planning process, only see half the of the strategic management equation. A fundamentally significant difference exists between strategic planning and strategic management. Strategic planning includes setting a vision, a mission, objectives, and strategies to achieve those objectives. Strategic management includes all of strategic planning *plus* the execution of a plan and a control for end results. If a plan isn't used to guide decisions and resource allocations, strategic management has not taken place. If a plan is used to guide decisions but little or no effort is made to ensure that performance is in line with the plan (particularly the achievement of strategic goals and objectives), strategic management is only partially fulfilled.

When seen in this light—that strategic management is more than just strategic planning—the challenge facing universities is heightened. Higher education needs to be operating two levels higher with respect to strategic management than where it has been over the past decades. It isn't good enough to simply create a strategic plan; that type of thinking reflects a very ancient approach to higher education. Yet this is where many in the university community are with respect to the management of their institutions—their ivory tower is above all of this management sleight of hand. Strategic planning and strategic management are what businesses do because they try to earn profits. In universities we don't dirty our hands with these base corporate-centric motives.

Due to the fact that universities face a decidedly uncertain environment, they should diligently implement strategic management processes to ensure that they successfully navigate the tumultuous waters. It is appropriate to review the essential ingredients comprising strategic management before considering how it should be implemented in the higher education context.

THE STRATEGIC MANAGEMENT PROCESS

Strategic management involves setting direction for an organization, executing strategies (or action plans), and controlling for deficiencies in organizational performance. In contrast, operational management addresses the daily details of implementing strategies and instituting continuous improvements to ensure attainment of high performance. The difference between these two responsibilities is perspective. Strategic management is concerned with the overall direction of an organization, and operational management is concerned with factors involved in reaching that intended path.

Ideally, every person within an organization is engaged in some aspect of strategic management. Personnel play an important role in day-to-day operations, but they also should contribute to their organization's evolving direction. Translating this to a university environment, faculty and staff have specific job responsibilities that they fulfill each day—their contribution to operational management. Additionally, they determine whether goals are achieved and whether chosen strategies should be modified to accomplish better performance.

This may come as a surprise to faculty and staff (i.e., that they should be involved in strategic management). After all, isn't that why administrators are paid huge salaries? Don't administrators ultimately determine where a university should head and how it will get there? In fact, administrators should encourage broad input from throughout a university about its future direction. Ultimately, top administrators are responsible for taking wide-ranging feedback and incorporating it within inspiring strategies and goals. But they cannot execute strategy without cooperation and buy-in from the vast number of faculty and staff members, who deliver classes, run the dorms, keep the heat and air conditioning flowing, and otherwise provide daily services that students, alumni, and the community expect.

Even the most strident staff or faculty members who insist that they have no role to play whatsoever in strategic management are by virtue of their refusal essentially partaking in the strategic management process. In essence, they have relinquished the opportunity to provide input about how their university can do a better job of delivering its services. Vital insights they possess may not be communicated to those who ultimately set strategy. These lost insights could make a difference in whether strategy is modified or left unchanged. When a university's strategy is out of synch with what customers and stakeholders expect, potential arises for students to enroll elsewhere, alumni to donate money to other causes, funding agencies to select grant applications from other institutions, and the football team to attract second-rate talent, among other potential malfunctions.

In sum, everyone in a university has a contribution to make to the strategic management of their organization. That doesn't necessarily mean that they will play a significant role or provide meaningful input, but that does not diminish their potential contribution.

Thompson and Strickland (1999) characterize the tasks of strategic management as follows:

1. *Forming a strategic vision of what the company's future business makeup will be and where the organization is headed—so as to*

provide long-term direction, delineate what kind of enterprise the company is trying to become, and infuse the organization with a sense of purposeful action.

2. *Setting objectives*—converting the strategic vision into specific performance outcomes for the company to achieve.
3. *Crafting a strategy to achieve the desired outcomes.*
4. *Implementing and executing the chosen strategy efficiently and effectively.*
5. *Evaluating performance and initiating corrective adjustments in vision, long-term direction, objectives, strategy, or implementation in light of actual experience, changing conditions, new ideas, and new opportunities.*

The relevance of Thompson and Strickland's definition of strategic management for higher education is that strategic planning alone—setting vision, mission, objectives, and strategy—does not fulfill the tasks of strategic management.

Strategic management is the wholesale involvement of people in articulating a university's direction, an action plan for getting there, and careful monitoring of performance so that intended goals and objectives are attained. The proportion of university and higher education leaders who understand these important differences is unclear. But one thing is certain: They need to be fully conversant and operationally adept in strategic management for their organizations to address challenges before them.

The Folly of Paying Lip Service to Strategic Management

The inability of some university leaders to move up a level from strategic planning to strategic management was driven home to me in a discussion I had with another dean from the East. She was snickering almost silently to herself during a conference workshop on mission-driven operations by our accrediting body. She shook her head, softly muttered several words before gaining composure, and then sat more attentively, focused on the speaker. Another PowerPoint slide flew across the screen landing on one emphasizing that budgets should be linked to strategic objectives, strategies, and tactics. At this she almost burst out laughing, but somehow drawing strength from deep within, she managed to stifle an outburst. She shook her head while tears formed in her eyes.

When break time neared I just had to find out what was so funny. Unquestionably she was having a good laugh and I needed a bit of humor given the boringly stale session we were sitting through. Around the refreshment table I sidled over and introduced myself. At first she was somewhat embarrassed that I had noticed her reaction. Then, without warning, she just started laughing almost uncontrollably. Finally, gaining composure, she was able to talk again and shared a most amazing story.

Her belief in the importance of strategic planning was unwavering, but the manner in which it was being implemented at her university did not make any sense. Almost five years ago her new president and provost decided to launch a strategic planning process. It was years since the university's strategic plan had been updated; not that anyone really noticed. Academic units simply went about their business as they pleased because the strategic plan was never referred to in any meaningful way. *There was no tangible link with the budget.*

To a large degree, the dean didn't contest the university's recent fascination with strategic planning and the tremendous resources being invested in updating the plan. However, her school already possessed a functional strategic plan that was periodically reviewed and revised. Annually she led department chairs in analyzing progress toward their strategic objectives. Performance gaps were noted and strategies revised to get back on track. Perhaps the school's plan wasn't perfect, nor was the execution and subsequent review of results, but at least faculty, staff, and students had an idea about where the school intended to go.

She looked wistfully distant for a moment and then told me that a vibrant strategic management effort at her university could potentially constrain her unit's strategic plan. It might set boundaries limiting the school's flexibility in setting vision, mission, and strategic objectives. Strategies to address competitive programs could also be adversely influenced. She contemplated several programs that might become expendable given the philosophical tendencies of faculty and administration on her campus. So strategic planning by the university carried some negative overtones.

Laughing lightly, she indicated that any cause for concern evaporated almost immediately when she saw how top leadership restructured the university's strategic planning process. For one thing, the new president virtually abdicated his participation in the planning process. He turned it over to the provost, who jumped in feet first with a relish. The poor provost didn't realize that many on the campus interpreted the president's lack of involvement as a signal to pay lip service to the planning process and its outcomes.

Thinking that everyone was on board, the provost established a complex planning process guided by an overarching task force. After an initial environmental scan (an exercise in the obvious, according to perceptive faculty and staff), fifteen committees were created to draft statements about potential strategic directions for the university. This process consumed *a year*. It ambitiously incorporated individuals—students, faculty, staff, and administrators—from throughout the campus while reaching deeply into the community for input. All appeared to be well and good, although the process was losing steam after eight months.

As even naïve members of the university community knew, the most decisive element of the strategic plan was defining key preeminent areas for the university. What academic programs, programmatic efforts, or interdisciplinary efforts would receive the highest priority and the most resources? In the end, that's what the strategic planning process was all about. Where will resources be directed to encourage growth and distinction? Or, as most viewed the process rather cynically, whose program would be targeted for downsizing or termination? Whose ox would be gored and whose would be fed?

The next four months of the strategic planning process centered around various task force meetings to solicit input on the strategic directions. It took far too long to identify proposed strategic directions, but in the end a list of seven directions was published. Not surprisingly, these strategic directions were overly broad and non-threatening. Every program on campus could lay claim to being part of a strategic direction involving research, students, or teaching.

More alarming was the definition of *more than 200* tactics to achieve the university's numerous strategic objectives. It was simply too much to cognitively integrate. Things began to fall apart in the planning process. Faculty, staff, and students kept looking to the president and provost for direction. Someone had to make a decision regarding what the university would be known for—its set of strategically important programs that distinguished it from other comparable institutions, its *brand*.

Almost five years after beginning the strategic planning process with such a flourish, virtually no further progress had been made. No one knew which academic programs were most important to the university. This was also a way of saying no one knew which programs were expendable. *No demonstrable linkage had been made with the budget.* Each year a new budget would roll out, and at the last moment someone would raise the question of how the strategic plan and budget were related.

Out of range from the president's and provost's hearing, the strategic plan became affectionately know as "Alice" (the true name has been changed as a matter of common decency). The university continued to muddle along without any constructive plan to guide resource deployment, and without accountability people quickly forgot all about the 200 tactics, objectives, and rationale for measuring performance in the first place.

My new friend the dean found immense consolation in the ability to continue steering her school where she and her stakeholders preferred. The university's strategic plan was essentially a sham, a faded memory to poke fun at. So when the conference presenter from the accrediting body pontificated about linking budgets with strategic objectives, strategy, and tactics, she could no longer contain herself. It might work via PowerPoint on a screen, but it would never see the light of day at her home institution.

There are several valuable lessons to be learned from this dean. First, for strategic planning to be comprehensively embraced across campus, it must be unequivocally backed by top leaders. Paying lip service will result in a similar return. Trustees, presidents, and provosts cannot delegate away the formation of a strategic plan or its implementation. They ultimately determine whether the university embraces a strategic plan and its implementation.

Second, this scenario indicates the importance of moving expeditiously in forming a strategic plan and incorporating broad input from diverse constituents. People's attention will wander quite quickly. Therefore, act decisively in establishing a streamlined process incorporating good representation both internally and externally. It should be a process that moves forward purposefully in crafting a final product. Not everyone will agree with a plan. They certainly won't agree if it never materializes.

Third, leaders must make decisions. They may not want to offend a certain segment of the university or community. But rest assured that cowardice in deciding what is and is not important as far as strategic direction represents the kiss of death for strategic planning. If university leaders fail to step up to the plate with bold and confident statements of direction, it should not be surprising that they find their institutions drifting merrily along headed toward a thousand different destinations.

Let's look at an alternative approach, a case where strategic planning led to a definitive statement and vision that an entire university and community was able to get behind.

Strategic planning can also be accomplished with flourishing ingenuity while widely embracing the entire gamut of academic stakeholders. In terms of implementation process and outcome, the following example—let's call this Alpha University—demonstrates the exact opposite compared to the situation covered above. This illustration of strategic planning finesse in a public university barely consumed more than a year from start to completion. That's a startling contrast to having two years slip by without any substantive progress other than wasting people's time and energy in a misconceived journey to confusion.

Alpha University began its invigorating drive toward a fresh new future when it hired a dynamic new president from a distant state. Her credentials were impeccable both as an academic and an experienced business professional. She was at a point in her career where it could all come together in a crescendo of excitement—the right president for the right setting with the right ingredients. Her mission was also crystal clear: Convert Alpha University from a lazy little feel-good campus with no real appeal (other than ease of access to community residents) or educational rigor into a driving force consonant with sparkling growth occurring throughout the area.

The new president's first move was to hire a new provost who also brought a fresh perspective and commitment to improvement as well as her own style and ideas about reinvigorating the university. Together the remarkable team of the president and provost made this whole strategic planning initiative work. They went together like peanut butter and jelly.

Such a charge was entirely plausible because major academic competition—primarily public institutions—languished some

200 miles away. This small city, with its agriculturally based economy, could use Alpha University as a catalyst toward greatness among communities throughout America. Sibling state universities had become lazy and fat. Their enrollments were dropping off as students flocked to Alpha University's mellow campus and far more interesting job prospects associated with the diversified economy of this quaint, but ambitious, town—a soon-to-be-favored destination for innovative technology businesses. Destiny waited for Alpha University to launch this humble little burg into rising star quality.

Everyone associated with Alpha University gulped big time as the president led off her administration with an announcement of a new strategic vision and the provost followed by launching the strategic planning effort. How many times had they been through that exercise in futility before to no avail? Not surprisingly this predictable pronouncement was greeted by a vast chorus of yawns. Senior faculty members set aside time on their calendars for a few more hands of bridge at the faculty club or an extra day each week for exercise. Most faculty members had begun to check out even before the president had discovered where her washroom was located. It was an overly anticipated, highly predictable beginning for a presidency except for one important difference. This time Alpha University's new president would define the vision herself. Then she would let a small provost-led group act as a guerilla team to flesh out an overall architecture before integrating other constituents.

Most at Alpha University didn't quite know how to react to this newfangled initiative. They were too accustomed to presidents administering rather than acting like executives. As faculty huddled in well-worn hallways and moldy offices across campus, a distinct buzz consumed conversations. Given this decisive leadership initiative, if they weren't careful, Alpha's new hard-charging president would get out too far in front of them and they might never rein her back in. Certainly faculty wanted a better university, but not at the expense of changing anything other than their salaries and teaching support.

Within several weeks, the president defined her vision: Alpha University would become "an inspired center of learning for the region." Faculty members stopped dead in their tracks. They were anticipating what had become a highly conventional pronouncement among this nation's universities about an institution devoted to leading research, service, and teaching. Almost in formulaic fashion, other colleges and universities espoused vision statements that upheld the holy trinity of teaching, research, and service or, at a very minimum, the sanctity of teaching and research. An emphasis on research had become a given—most universities desperately needed research funding to support graduate students and provide supplemental income to faculty, especially during the long, hot summers in Alpha's hometown.

Academic leaders and colleagues crammed the faculty club and student union in clutches of heated discussion. If research wasn't incorporated in the vision, then how could they possibly justify course release time? Every faculty member, except the most dim-witted, could present a façade of respectable research—a study, manuscript, or data collection effort that justified release from a portion of their class loads. This aggressive initiative by the president was completely in line with community and student complaints. Students had expressed concern that faculty members were too busy doing research to meet with them. A few powerful voices in the community argued that faculty members were disconnected from real life; faculty expertise was seldom translated into any tangible benefit for the community. Whether this was true or not, many speculated that it had led in part to the ouster of Alpha University's last president.

While faculty and staff members pontificated in the halls and gathering places of Alpha University, the president went on the offensive. She asked the provost to assemble six to eight good minds to structure the planning process and to operationally define "an inspired center of learning for the region." This group was unofficially labeled "the Gang of 8." Over the next seven months it would aid in fine-tuning the vision and corresponding mission statement, conduct internal focus groups (of approximately thirty different focus group meetings with hundreds of participants) and forums about the planning process, select the strategic planning team (of approximately forty members), assist in data collection, and prepare for the next step in the process of organizing goals and strategies based on feedback.

The planning team was given several weeks (at the end of the Gang of 8's seven-month period) to review and agree on the next steps in the planning process, review and refine the definition of the vision, discuss and agree on a framework for data collection, and acquire additional desired data. The planning team was comprised of forty representatives drawn from among deans, department chairs, staff, student leaders, and faculty. Their main job was to seek input on what "an inspired center of learning for the region" means to faculty, staff, students, businesses, and the community. By this point the president had clearly communicated within the university and community her expectations for achieving "an inspired center of learning" over the course of her term.

Some would criticize this process because it may not have given sufficient opportunity for penetrating, wide-ranging discussion and feedback about the vision. On the one hand, the process appeared to be too rushed and driven from the top down. On the other hand, the president should be congratulated for her decisiveness—a quality sorely lacking in prior administrations. Her bold statement and energetic work to personally encourage the rest of the academic community to get on board proved to be infectious. The strategic planning team concentrated on collecting additional feedback about the vision from external and internal stakeholders.

Following data collection, the hard-working Group of 8 and planning team of forty went through an intense period of give and take in the planning process. Together they distilled external constituent feedback into detailed refinements of what the vision meant and what the implications were for goals and strategies. They launched a six-month collaborative effort to draft action steps, target dates, and responsible parties (for accomplishing actions and goals) while simultaneously seeking feedback on the vision, mission, goals, and strategies from faculty, staff, advisory boards (within the university and colleges), and students. Subsequently a set of strategic university priorities was drafted in addition to articulating a process for college and division plans to align with the overall university plan.

Following this data collection period, the planning team met two more times to review and refine goals, strategies, and actions, begin the definition of key performance indicators, discuss the integration of division and college planning outcomes, finalize strategic priorities, collect input on implementation issues, and discuss documentation and monitoring.

In the final two months, the provost tightly monitored the final preparation of the strategic plan. Internal and external documents were drafted and discussed prior to fine-tuning. Plans were laid for presentation to the planning team and the state's board of education. Groundwork was begun to tie plans to the budgeting process. As a result, colleges that best linked their plans with the overarching university plan were positioned to do better in the budgeting process.

The process launched colleges into their own strategic planning process and wisely accommodated the reality that each college would follow its own pace. This flexibility facilitated a growing willingness by faculty to join in strategic planning and to define a tempo favorable to each college. In many respects this initiative created a bottom-up quality to Alpha University's overall strategic planning. College-wide and university-wide strategic planning began to meld seamlessly as a common language and visionary focus permeated the campus.

Over the course of some sixteen months, Alpha University eventually owned a new strategic plan tied to college plans and loosely integrated with the budgeting process. Over the following year refinements were instilled throughout the plan and especially to coordination with budgeting processes. Across campus, most faculty and staff admitted that they had been given sufficient opportunity to have their say. With the president's charismatic and visionary leadership, Alpha University simply moved forward. It wasted little time due to rancor regarding fine nuances associated with the vision of "an inspired center of learning for the region." An iterative top-down/bottom-up process ensured opportunities for all to have input who chose to provide their insights.

A very tangible product from this journey in strategic planning was a one-page encapsulated overview of the strategic plan on a "Z-Card." Administrators, faculty, staff, students, and stakeholders could carry around the entire strategic plan on a folding document the size of a business card bloated by steroids. One side of the document defines the destination and milestones for measuring progress and goals. The flip side incorporates a strategy matrix, matching goals with strategies. The portability of this strategic plan has been extremely beneficial in ensuring that it is a functional tool and continually referenced throughout university operations, budgeting, and long-run thinking. Not surprisingly the portable Z-Card plan has also served as a convenient form of effective communication to external constituents.

Prior to the strategic plan leaders within the university were seeking budget supplements all year long from the provost with little linkage to an overarching strategic direction. Once the plan was in place, the budget process was modified to a once-a-year event where all new budget initiatives were tied explicitly to strategic goals. When Alpha University launched a comprehensive campaign, the strategic plan served as a convenient structure for identifying key fundraising initiatives. As Alpha University undertook a comprehensive review of all centers and institutes, the strategic plan again served as a framework for assessment.

Alpha University didn't fool itself into thinking that it had developed a foolproof plan. To this day, the plan continues to be updated and adjusted according to the latest circumstances and achievements. More progress needs to be made on the connection between planning and budgeting. However, for once Alpha University has consensus on where it is going and how it will get there. Little bumps along the way may prevent this hallowed institution from making progress as fast as the president or provost wish, but the strategic plan remains a guide to decision-making and improvement. It sets a foundation for the entire university and community to build what will become a most respected center of learning in its region.

The two completely different models for strategic planning illustrated in this chapter suggest a significant difference: a well-articulated and widely embraced plan is vastly powerful for moving an institution of higher learning forward toward prominence.

THE IMPERATIVE TO FOCUS

Since the 1980s, U.S.-based organizations have become acutely sensitive to rising national and global competition. There is at least one significant lesson not-for-profit organizations and corporations have learned during the intervening halcyon days that is exceptionally apropos to universities. The last two decades have taught enterprises the inherent value of focusing their missions, objectives, and strategies. Far fewer firms are now highly diversified. If they have maintained a diversified strategy, they tend to follow a path of related diversification to capitalize on synergies in functions such as marketing or production.

Corporations concentrate on creating competitive strategies—devising plans of action to beat competitors, to win market share, to reap the highest profitability, and to become top dog in their industry. It's all about establishing a recognizable brand and competitive strategy, the obsession of savvy corporations. Firms are finding better ways to hone strategies at serving customers, building products, relating with suppliers, informing capital markets about their performance, and creating a promising foundation for successful business in the future.

At the same time, strategic management is becoming democratized. Personnel at all levels can offer input regarding strategy adjustments. For example, a staff member responsible for purchasing various electronic components may catch a glimpse of a market opportunity. Or, she may see a way to reduce inventory carrying costs that can literally save hundreds of thousands, if not millions, of dollars. Her ability to share these insights with top management and their openness to her suggestions imply a collaborative relationship among employers and employees.

The repercussions of the corporate strategy revolution for higher education are considerable. However, higher education is fighting pressures that the private sector has, for the most part, successfully negotiated. Our universities, particularly public institutions, have not wanted to make the same kinds of internal transformations observed in business.

As astute leaders have painfully learned, you cannot build and sustain great programs (or products and services) these days through an excessively broad focus— being everything to everyone. You must create a distinctive brand. Yet, this breadth is precisely what most state-funded universities are trying to preserve. They see their mission and vision as being full service when in fact resource support and student demand argue otherwise. Philosophically, many would rather close their doors than cut a single program because they rationalize that all programs are needed to serve the public interest.

Sadly, intellectual elitism may encourage resistance to doing what is right from a strategic management perspective. We couldn't possibly continue as an institution without a full-service languages department. What type of university would people think we have if we cut the renaissance arts and music technology departments? And the athletics program? Alumni would scream if we cut back to four sports instead of twelve. We may not be competitive in any of the sports, but at least we are fielding teams that go to the slaughter.

GENERIC STRATEGY OPTIONS

Universities can select from a number of strategies without all looking like they were made from the same cookie cutter. The strategic management literature indicates that five generic strategies are available to any organization:

From these generic options flow all manner of specialized interpretations that embody a focused mission, objectives, and strategies.

Not every university can chase the same strategy and still be recognized for excellence. There are choices to be made. Perhaps a college's resources are best focused (i.e., a niche strategy) on serving a particular type, or niche, of student—students with exceptional intelligence but low ambition, students with learning challenges, or students who coasted through high school and never lived up to their potential but now are prepared to commit fully to a rigorous course of study.

Alternatively, a university may strive to produce the highest quality degree at the lowest cost—a best value strategy. This approach would guide decisions such as student admissions. Only the most capable students among those applying would be

Strategy Option	Definition
Low Cost Leadership	Strive to produce the lowest cost education/degree
Niche	Serve a specific target group of students
Broad Differentiation	Serve a broad academic market by offering many degree programs
Focused Low Cost	Serve a narrow target group of students with a specific cost advantage
Best Value	Deliver the highest-quality education at the lowest cost

admitted. This strategy differs significantly from one of providing the lowest-cost education where admissions are wide open. Under a best value strategy, admissions are more selective.

A broad differentiation strategy, a path that many public universities follow, attempts to serve a broad academic market by offering many degree programs. Nonetheless, only a limited handful of universities can achieve excellent performance in delivering full-service academic programs. Continuing intensive funding is required to build and sustain uniformly high quality academic programs. Unfortunately, many states fall short in their ability to feed this strategy due to fiscal and resource constraints.

A focused low-cost strategy serves students in a niche at the lowest possible cost. For example, a business school might initiate an executive master of business administration (EMBA) degree program serving students with five years of business experience who are on an upward managerial track. The school attempts to attract students by offering the lowest price EMBA degree program. The academic quality of this program would probably resemble many of the more expensive competitors, but associated amenities (e.g., curriculum innovation, high-tech classrooms, dedicated staff, meals, etc.) would be curtailed to keep delivery costs (and price) at the lowest level.

As the generic competitive strategies suggest, there is more than one way to achieve a distinctive strategy in higher education and more than one way to build a distinctive brand. Universities basically need to approach their choice of strategies with greater discretion, allowing for new articulations of vision and mission. Not every university should be a full-service provider; only a few universities can expect to achieve international recognition for balancing teaching and research. The challenge is to craft a mission, strategic objectives, and set of strategies appropriate to the existing and feasible strengths of a university—a redefinition of identity that many are not bold enough to tackle, though exceptions can be found.

THE INHERENT BEAUTY OF DEFINING WHO YOU ARE

One early spring day a handful of colleagues and I attended a workshop on strategic planning for business schools. You would think that most business schools have their acts together as far as their strategic plans, wouldn't you? But in truth, faculties are faculties, whether they are in the business school or East Asian languages department. Actually, business school faculties may be worst in this regard because they fight over the slightest nuance.

During a break I was talking with two faculty members from a medium-sized Southern college. The session had just concluded with a boisterous discussion about business school missions. Most of the attendees who shared their mission statements talked about lofty aspirations for excellence in teaching, research, and service. Surprisingly, teaching schools also pandered to research in the breadth of their mission statements. This herd mentality seemed forgivable. Accreditation standards specifically called for the production of intellectual contributions even from schools whose missions are inherently teaching in orientation.

Finally, one of the two faculty members with whom I was sharing a spot of tea read his school's proposed mission statement. They were in the very middle of the process of refining their mission. It was the initial sentence that took my breath away: "We're just the Canella Institute . . . ." He went on to recite a mission that emphasized teaching and preparation of students for careers (rather than jobs) and a productive life. Not one word was devoted to research.

"We're just X or Y . . . ." How refreshing it would be if more universities admitted what the rest of us know about them—they can make no claim to excellence in research nor will they ever be able to. They can't even make a good case for excellence in teaching. Without a question they cannot make a claim for excellence in teaching, research, and service. They simply do not have the firepower to achieve excellence in two or more areas. They may not have enough resources to aspire to greatness in even one area.

In reality, few private universities can become Harvard or Stanford, and few public universities can become a Michigan or a Berkeley. Nonetheless, every university can be renowned for one or several programs. It's all a matter of focus and living bigger on a budget no matter how modest it may be. But you can't get there by refusing to look internally. You will never reach greatness by failing to focus resources and avoiding dialogues regarding vision, mission, objective, and strategies as a prelude to actual transformation.

Focus in university missions, objectives, and strategies becomes a metaphor for greatness and reputation for owning a superlative brand. Excessively broad statements and aspirations (relative to resource base) only lead to mediocrity. Second-rate status is unfortunately what many universities are driving toward as the resource and funding landscape around them changes, as they refuse to create adaptive responses commensurate with these changes. University leaders—specifically regents and trustees—benignly tolerate the failure of top academic administrators to lead their institutions out of mediocrity because of the fundamentally painful revolution that will occur.

No president or provost, much less regent or trustee, wants to see a campus in turmoil under their watch. So it is much easier to tweak a little here or there and sell these modest changes as transformation when they really are only palliative. They have observed other organizations' experiences in order-of-magnitude transformations with the widespread human grief resulting when masses of personnel are terminated. What academic leader wants to go through such an exercise? Certainly regents and trustees aren't paid enough—or anything—to go through that. And how is a president or provost going to move to a better position through a legacy of right-sizing?

In the final analysis we will only build a better system of higher education by focusing scarce resources. It's time for universities to make the tough choices—to cut out the mediocre business school and to reinvest in the already prominent biology department, to close down the languishing geography department and reinvest in the math department, or to shut down all doctoral programs turning out second-rate scholars and reinvest in master's programs.

Clearly many in academia will see the preceding admonitions as heresy. They might argue that such recommendations are business-centric drivel, not worthy of consideration in esteemed university halls. Others will agree with a call to focus, so long as it's the other departments or schools/colleges on campus that take the hit. This is academic cowardice at its worst. Those in corporations and many in the public sector whose organizations and industries have already gone through a revolution—already experienced the pain and travail—will not be the least bit sympathetic.

The great opportunity before higher education with respect to focus is *the chance to lead evolution and to prevent revolution*. Wait any longer and higher education's reluctance to instill change will stimulate a call from legislatures, taxpayers, and alumni to not only tighten the belt but to completely change the emperor's clothes. Wouldn't it be nice if academic leaders actually led for a change by initiating processes to focus their programs or by terminating mediocre academic enclaves, reinvesting in promising academic initiatives and in the process producing a much higher return on resources invested?

EFFECTIVELY IMPLEMENTING STRATEGIC MANAGEMENT

Aggressively pursuing a strategy for distinction and building a unique brand imply leadership from top echelons in making tough calls. Academic administrators have to do a better job of leading by making strategic decisions after receiving requisite input. They also must ensure that strategic management processes are credible to maintain widespread support. Effective implementation is easier said than done as the following vignette illustrates.

I was bone-tired, having slaved intensely for three weeks collecting data and information, massaging the figures, and drafting sections of our plan only to redo them for what seemed the thousandth time. The school's strategic plan and budget request would be presented to the council of deans next week. The dean and I were determined to present an unequivocally compelling case for additional resources. The strength of this presentation could ultimately determine whether resources would be forthcoming to continue our growth trajectory. Too tired to care anymore, I just wanted this pathetic strategic planning exercise to be over.

Our planning assumptions were quite explicit. The provost wanted us to present two scenarios—operations under a 10 percent budget reduction and expanded operations under a 10 percent budget increase. We had to identify what would be sliced if our funding was decreased. Among other questions we were tasked to address: (1) What choices would we make in terms of sacrificing academic programs and how would this affect our drive toward distinctiveness?, (2) How would our choices affect students and the ability to serve our research, teaching, and service missions?, (3) What new programs, if any, would be added with a 10 percent larger pie?, (4) Would the additional funding simply buttress what was already in place?, and (5) Did we anticipate any internal reallocations under either scenario? The provost emphasized that strategic planning was central to moving this university forward.

Fortunately, our school had been methodically working on its strategic plan, otherwise this would have been a total nightmare. We had already informed the faculty and taken the matter to the school's equivalence of an operations and strategic planning committee. Not surprisingly, the committee indicated that the deans (i.e., the dean and associate dean) could prepare drafts and then it would make requisite changes to the final document. That, of course, translated to me doing all the work. But that's the life of an associate dean.

I could only cringe at what must be happening in units that hadn't developed a strategic plan. Most likely those deans never even bothered to integrate faculty into the exercise, perhaps not even keep them informed. "What the faculty don't know won't hurt them" seemed to be the thinking of most of my colleague deans. Such an approach would make this exercise easier. Unfortunately, that's not the reality I faced. Now, where did I put those statistics on burgeoning enrollment growth?

Three interminable days later, the dean inferred that we were about there in completing our plan. The draft and accompanying narrative met all of the key criteria specified by the provost. The faculty's planning committee seemed to accept the direction our dean's presentation would take. There had been some tussling over allocating additional resources to the finance and technology management department, but a peaceful accord soon followed. Besides, everyone knew that probabilities favored a budget reduction since the state was facing serious revenue shortfalls.

After several hours trying to improve two statistical tables, I couldn't stand it any longer and walked down the hall toward the mailroom to see if anything new had arrived in this afternoon's bundle. I really had to give credit to my assistant. Her timing was impeccable. She saw this freight train coming and decided to take annual leave this week when all of the report preparation would be finalized.

I passed three colleagues huddled in an animated conversation. Near-shouting by one tailed off as I walked by. Guilty glances looked my way. Only one verbally acknowledged my presence with a barely audible, "Hi." I thought to myself: "Hey friends, chill out. I already know the scuttlebutt in the hallways is quite critical of the dean's proposals that he will be putting forward. I'm guilty by association; I know that."

Ninety minutes later I slipped the report in the dean's mailbox and snuck out the back door. He would continue to make changes until the final hour, why encourage him by being available? Dog needs to go for a walk and I want to feel like I'm actually living a life, not earning a living.

The following Monday afternoon, my boss had me accompany him to his presentation before the provost and deans. He was a bit nervous about explaining some of the data. I was the true repository of the information and knew the detail; he didn't. But, that's the way we worked together to our mutual satisfaction. He saw the big picture—the forest—and I saw the small picture—the trees. I was there merely as a lifeline, but he was a seasoned pro. He wouldn't be calling on me, so I took a comfortable seat off to the side with other directors, staff, and lower deans. This would be a relaxing hour while my boss did his magic.

It was a very impressive performance; worthy of an Academy Award for drama and emotional delivery. He had them eating out of his hand and then oh-so-subtly laid out an inarguable plea for significant resources. To my surprise, he shot the moon and went for a 15 percent increase. That took them by surprise. But the clincher was his story about one of our graduates who grew up in orphanages and as a single mother fought her way to a bachelor's degree. She's now earning good money in a plum position with a prominent local firm. There's no question that her child will go on to earn her degree—that's the difference our school makes in the lives of others.

Even I had tears in my eyes. He told a simple, truthful, powerful story in putting this puppy to bed. I noticed a number of the deans wipe their eyes surreptitiously, and I heard a muffled sob behind me. Several in the audience had taken tissues out and were blowing their noses or dabbing their eyes. Wow. But I kept focused on the provost's reaction. He must have a heart of stone. He just sat there unflinchingly twiddling a paperclip, almost with a look of boredom—the cad. Heartlessness must be a prime requisite for candidates to that job. Oh well, I can take my leave at the break after the next dean presents.

My dean came back to the office after the council was through. I was obediently waiting for a debriefing. Seems everyone's presentation was a plea for additional resources. He felt we made a good case, and I congratulated him on the delivery. It was absolutely first-rate. The dean from arts and sciences made an unusually abbreviated pitch, so we speculated on what that might mean.

Eventually the conversation focused on the provost and his reaction to the presentations. Agreement suggested that the provost didn't really seem to be there in an alert, concentrated way. He appeared to be distracted and was continually glancing at papers that he had in front of him. It's impossible to read what's on his mind. More than likely we will know the outcome from the exercise within the next week.

Well, the next week came and went without avail. The dean received no call from the provost, and our best internal sources of clandestine information in the provost's office didn't throw any bones our way. At our faculty's planning meeting the following week, the dean replayed his presentation and the pitch for an additional budget increase of 15 percent. This had everyone feeling good and quite optimistic. But there still wasn't as much as a peep out of the provost's office.

Semester break came before I knew it, and suddenly we were three months out from that period of hell in preparing the fiscal planning document and incorporating faculty input. The old admonition of "hurry up and wait" appeared to rule once again. Not so much as a whisper had been passed down from on high. Sources suggested that an announcement would be forthcoming in the next two weeks, but that was the only information that had been shared.

Some weeks later the dean returned from the council of deans meeting with a shell-shocked look on his face. I braced for the inevitable—our school would be taking a 10 percent hit.

No, that wasn't quite it.

The dean could hardly speak he was so mad—it seemed that the provost had made a very short cursory announcement at the end of the meeting. He thanked everyone for their hard work and the high quality of the presentations. He thought it was a good planning exercise and a hugely important discussion. However, reallocation was simply too divisive an option to implement. He had decided that there would be no budget reductions or increases—no changes whatsoever.

If ever there was a textbook case in how not to encourage strategic planning, the preceding vignette certainly meets the criteria of a perfect example. Faculty throughout university campuses are pretty jaded by strategic planning efforts. They have watched too many resources be invested in lengthy efforts to set direction, only to have plans ignored or subsequently trashed by a new incoming administration. Given the propensity of presidents and provosts to move on to bigger and better positions, there is a high tendency for planning initiatives by many administrations to never see full execution.

The very last thing we need in higher education is continued cynicism about strategic plans, the failure of top leaders to make tough decisions, and a paralyzed strategic management process because no one cared enough to lead our universities and colleges to greatness. By the same token we can no longer afford mediocrity in higher education if this nation is to become a more humane and enlightened society intending to help other countries become the same. Leading through strategic management is the beginning from which we travel down this long and dusty road.

Chapter 4

HIGHEST AND BEST
USE OF RESOURCES

One afternoon I received an urgent call from the chancellor's assistant apologizing for the extremely late notice, but an emergency meeting of the chief of police, vice president for business affairs, deans, myriad associate provosts, and key administrative leaders had been called for early the next morning at 8:00 A.M.

"Would you be able to clear your calendar to make the meeting?"

"Sure thing," I replied, "but why are we starting so late in the morning if it's that urgent?"

"Oh you know, that's actually very early for everyone over here in this building [the university's central administrative complex]."

"OK, I'll be there, but is there anything I can do to prepare for the meeting?"

"No; just show up."

I hung up the phone and leaned back in my chair emitting a long, loud mournful sigh. Wonder what it is this time? Drop everything and come running because we need to have an encompassing discussion. "Just show up." I think I can do that. But in reality, I had set aside three precious hours—6:00 A.M. to 9:00 A.M.—that morning to work on accreditation documents. After the call, I knew that I would be preparing those accreditation documents on Saturday afternoon after teaching that morning in our executive program.

I hurried over to a beat-up credenza and sorted through my "a, b, and c" piles. I had essentially just signed up to waste an hour-plus of quality time. But, 98 percent of all academic administrators see any meeting as a good meeting. I sensed that tomorrow's tête-à-tête would allow me to draft several innocuous memos that had been waiting in the "b and c" piles. It was now just a matter of selecting those for which limited brain power was required.

Like a card shark carefully drawing a winning hand, I pulled out items from the "b and c" piles and stacked them in order of intended completion. Don't want to make too much of a scene shuffling through this pile at the meeting. Got to keep it crisp, peeling off the top as each item is laid low.

Before the emergency meeting started, I would have been working on accreditation for an hour and a half. Consequently I must be disciplined and stop at exactly 7:35 A.M. because it takes ten minutes to walk to the conference room. I don't want to be late in selecting a seat. I'll sit at the far end of the massive table behind a physically tall dean who always has great insights and a humorous touch. This ploy will provide first-class physical coverage—screening—and some of those wise-old-owl comments my slim-Jim colleague makes may inadvertently be attributed to me. Perfect.

At 7:35 A.M. the next day, my plan is put in motion. Arriving in the conference room at exactly 7:45 A.M., I have my choice of seats. One mission accomplished, but can I pull off the others? For the next thirty minutes people dribble into the meeting. Why are so many people cavalier about being late? Do they know something I don't know? Not really; they just count on the chair of this meeting being his usual fifteen minutes late. Let's see, it's 8:14 A.M.—and here he comes.

The meeting proceeds to unfold. I listen attentively ready to shift modes when the inevitable circuitous discussion begins. It seems we have a big security crisis on our hands. This is of utmost importance to everyone's safety—students, faculty, staff, public, and administration. Then the pontificators take over. One blowhard after another agrees with the chancellor about the urgency of the problem and how it can have a major impact on their unit's operations. They wear little beatific smiles after speaking, proud of their allegiance to the number two top dog. Thirty-five minutes later when they run out of steam the chancellor steps up to the plate.

What did he just say?

Did I hear correctly?

The chancellor bluntly told us that a task force is already in place. And it's supposed to report to us at this meeting!

One of the three members forming the task force clears his throat uncomfortably. "We have been discussing the matter, but we don't have a plan of action firmed up yet. We anticipate having it ready later this afternoon."

Hello? You nincompoops didn't do your job? In industry you would be sent packing. And Mister Chair, why in the world didn't you verify this and cancel this morning's meeting? Damn.

The pontificators rise to the chancellor's defense, blowing about how vastly significant this issue is and how we need to nip it in the bud before someone gets hurt. Several inane ideas are thrown out by members of the task force in an attempt to recover, but the chair isn't going to be placated that easily. It's now 9:10 A.M. and I'm wondering why he doesn't simply terminate the meeting because the task force has nothing to report.

"Calm down," I tell myself. "Focus on writing your memos. You don't have a dog in this fight." Come to think of it, I'll actually enjoy Saturday afternoon with that warm sun streaming into my office, providing an angelic golden glow on the accreditation documents.

At 9:25 A.M. the chair announces that we will get together in two days to revisit the task force's report. Superficially, he appears wise in his ways, but I bet he gives someone a good chewing out over this faux pas.

I run back over to my office and try to take up where I left off, but my groove, a smooth flow, has been interrupted, and by now faculty and staff have come into work. Great to see them here bright and early! I tell myself to refocus. "Drat, a telephone call that I don't need." Seconds later the morning and petty demands wash over me, sweeping away any possibility of productive results.

Later that afternoon I take a moment to calculate the cost of the wasted emergency meeting. Let's assume that each of the thirty people spent 1.75 hours in travel time and meeting time to attend a non-event. Assume that the average salary cost of these high-level administrators is something around $90 per hour. Given these premises, the salary cost alone of the meeting was $4,725 without considering lost productivity. The chancellor had just blown almost $5,000 in taxpayer's' money. Gone in the blink of eye. But, did anyone really care? Probably not.

This vignette occurs time and time again in academia. It's illustrative of a sad malaise rampant throughout those ivy-covered halls. Few in the university setting have a sense of urgency about anything. The thinking tends to go as follows: "We are blessed with plenty of time. Whatever seems urgent isn't. It can wait until tomorrow. After all, we should discuss this properly. Wouldn't want to make a rash decision. Wouldn't want to make the wrong decision. Wouldn't want to make any decision."

Perhaps attitudes such as these are a byproduct of faculty governance—the cost paid for collegial decision-making. My faculty colleagues must have a consensus. They'll talk something to death before they capitulate to a decision in which a few aren't on board. Better to put off a decision in the fond hope that through further discourse they might browbeat someone into submission. Or there is always the prospect that their extraordinary oratory skills will finally sink through those impenetrable Neanderthal skulls of the opposition.

And so academics muddle through the day, the week, the month, and the academic year. Next thing they know, its mid-May and finals are approaching. No time left to make decisions or set important policy. It can wait until fall semester. It's too big an issue to discuss while everyone is off preparing their final exams. And, just like that, the semester is over and faculty members on nine-month contracts are off doing their research—out of state, out of the country, and out of mind.

THE CASE FOR BETTER RESOURCE STEWARDSHIP

Is this really any way to run a multimillion-dollar, a billion-dollar, a multibillion-dollar business? What's that you're thinking? Universities aren't businesses? Forget that naïve idea. Simply look at how many communities rely on colleges and universities as an economic engine. When viewed in this manner, it's clear that universities are essentially responsible for a major economic impact throughout our nation. Total state funding alone for higher education in fiscal year 2003 was $122.9 billion (NASBO, 2003). Now that's big business.

When looking at these enormous expenditures, it's a little easier to understand my anguish over meetings that go nowhere and that accomplish nothing. These daily habits reflect an encompassing moré about the value of time and the luxury academics have in expending that resource. A blasé attitude about time ultimately translates to blasé management of resources. Here's the rub as far as taxpayers are concerned: A proper sense of stewardship does not exist within ivy-covered halls.

If every faculty member and academic administrator treated their time as though they personally paid for it, if they treated their unit's budget as if it was their money, and if they treated university buildings, equipment, and other assets as though they held title to them, we would witness a dramatically different use of those assets. But the scale of things is so large—the responsibility so diluted—that there is no proper sense of stewardship.

This lackadaisical attitude is particularly aggravating to taxpayers because academics hold the public trust. Citizens pay lots of taxes to create, maintain, and grow institutions of higher education. They expect that these scarce resources will be treated like any other valuable asset—with due diligence and exceptional fiscal prudence. Yet the reality is higher education plays both the fool and the spendthrift offspring. Meanwhile the taxpayer watches as funds are continually squandered on poorly conceived programs, duplicated services and degree programs, inefficient staffing and abysmal productivity, low quality academic initiatives, pork projects, and fourth-rate athletic programs.

INCENTIVES AND IMPROVED RESOURCE STEWARDSHIP

Academic administrators and faculty members would possess an entirely different set of attitudes if they owned the resources. When a person owns a million dollars, it is more likely that she or he will do everything possible to make certain that the maximum value is earned on that sum of money. Of course, the concept of maximum value is open to definition. To one millionaire it might mean the highest annual interest. To another it may mean deriving the maximum number of luxury cruises. To another it may imply helping the highest number of homeless people.

Despite definitional problems, there is no argument that ownership of assets creates an entirely different set of expectations, behaviors, and attitudes surrounding how those assets are used. The problem in higher education is that we don't have enough people trying desperately to achieve the highest and best use of public resources. Too many academics and academic administrators treat resources under their care in a most cavalier way. It isn't that they necessarily misuse resources so much as they fail to passionately make certain that scarce resources are used wisely to produce the highest return.

What would happen if incentives were actually given to academic administrators when they demonstrated wise use of resources? Conceive of the scenario where the taxpayer essentially agrees that universities get to keep half of every dollar saved. Wouldn't this introduce the incentive to pursue widespread innovation? Would universities suddenly be able to serve more students on fewer dollars? Might there be fewer maintenance people because overnight the remaining more highly paid—incentivized—staff members are making heroic efforts to keep university facilities and grounds in tip-top shape? Wouldn't those lingering marginal academic programs be cut and saved resources reinvested in making strong programs better?

Unfortunately we can only speculate about how behavior would change if academics themselves received a cut of the action. But because academics are people, there is strong reason to believe that they would respond favorably to incentive systems.

Actually I did run across an interesting case of what happens under incentive plans in academia. Although such plans are rare, they do exist beyond the president, chief academic officer, and athletic department. I was attending an annual meeting in Los Angeles of the Association to Advance Collegiate Schools of Business–International where I joined a group of colleagues sharing tales from back home. Waiting for lunch to be served, I became quite intrigued with the fascinating tale the dean next to me was recounting about her executive director of external programs.

Many business schools offer external training, degree programs, and consulting through the arm of their external programs. These initiatives fulfill educational needs and serve as an extremely important source of additional revenue. When managed correctly, they can spin off a considerable amount of spare change that can be used for student and faculty support as well as seed funding for growing new programs.

In this particular instance the dean talked wistfully about how the executive director just could do nothing wrong in the first four years after joining the school and program. He doubled admissions to an executive MBA program, encouraged faculty to bring their consulting in-house, and grew the non-degree component. In fact, he was so successful in the non-degree arena that he hired an associate director to ramp up these offerings and capture more of the market. Before long, the associate director had doubled the amount of business coming through the doors.

It was a flurry of activity. Local corporations called wanting tailored training programs for staff. Non-degree certificate programs in basic management skills were selling out beyond all expectations. Faculty landed several major consulting programs. Times were flush, and money rolled in the door. Because the executive director was paid on an incentive basis, the higher the gross and net revenues, the larger was his incentive bonus. Driven by this allure of a healthy salary supplement each year, the executive director made certain that the dean received a sizeable sum to allocate among students and faculty. Life was good, very good.

But all good things must come to an end, and such was the case for this dean. She recounted how the vice president for business affairs simply would not leave well enough alone. The vice president hounded her about incentive payments to her executive director. "They were too large. What would the regents say if they found out? No one else receives these payments." Of course this wasn't quite true because the president, provost, and coaches all received incentive payments. The vice president enlisted the help of the provost and president to badger the dean about resolving the matter.

Finally, to be a good citizen and demonstrate to those above her that her school wanted what was best for the university as a whole, she capitulated. The dean agreed to convert the executive director to straight salary. In a show of good faith, appreciation, and loyalty, she increased the executive director's base by 50 percent. This was a very large increase, but human resources agreed with the conversion simply to terminate the incentive plan. Surely the dean had won a friend for life? Wrong.

The very next year the entire complexion of the external program operations changed. Suddenly more staff members were hired. It was rationalized by the executive and associate directors that the growth of the programs could only be fueled by investing more in program staffing. People were spread too thin. Sales were being lost because follow-up wasn't timely enough. Quality was beginning to erode. Not surprisingly, the next year the same sort of changes occurred. More staff members were added to cover this thriving business and to seek out additional contracts.

Overall, the non-degree program was growing rapidly and so was its cost structure. Although business more than doubled, profitability tanked. It now cost slightly more to offer the non-degree programs than was generated in revenue. The executive director and associate director rationalized that this wasn't a problem, because the non-degree programs attracted students to the more lucrative executive degree program. They argued that profitability from the non-degree programs could be found in the return generated elsewhere in external programs. It was a most impressive display of smoke and mirrors.

Without an incentive at play, the predictable happened. The executive director was no longer worried about building a large bottom line because he did not benefit from it. He was more interested in building a kingdom with lots of serfs to cater to his whims and needs. He gobbled up space whenever he could to house his minions in luxurious accommodations. His staff had the latest computer equipment and software, the plushest facilities, and the most cell phones. He strutted around his kingdom expecting total allegiance and throwing a tantrum whenever staff failed to kiss his ring.

And the poor dean? Her reward was less money to fund student scholarships. Faculty grew cranky because they were not receiving annual increases in research support. New programs were left on the back burner because seed funding had dried up. But that was her problem. The executive director had his high salary; tough luck for the dean who had given him such courtesy, treated him with such largesse.

In this example, central administration was operating from a philosophy that economic or financial incentives are inappropriate in a public management context. Well, that's not quite how they operate. As the dean shared, she suspected that the president, provost, and coaches were all receiving some sort of incentive, and she had heard rumors about fellow deans. Nonetheless, the expectation for academic units is that fiscal incentives are inappropriate. People serve in higher education because they believe in contributing to the common good. They receive their intrinsic reward from living a life of the mind. They don't sully themselves with base motivations such as money.

Without the incentive to deliver the highest and best use of resources invested, academia has devolved into a money pit. There is no widespread drive across university campuses to manage resources intelligently. Year after year, our fallback is a trip to the legislature with hands out asking for more money. And, when other programs beat us to the gate—prisons, health care, K-12 education, social services—we obediently wait on the sideline like good puppies waiting for our masters to come back next year with more chow.

The sad reality is that philosophically universities are dead set against operating like businesses. Great fear and trepidation surrounds anything that smacks of economic incentives. Faculty members abhor the "corporatization" of universities, where business practices are used to instill some fiscal sanity into resource use. We have gone too long operating under the same old premises. A cost-plus mentality has been inculcated throughout higher education. It continues at the very top echelons of university administration. Leaders simply perpetuate lazy attitudes about managing taxpayers' resources.

Opportunity Costs and Resource Stewardship

A colleague shared his story about the annual August retreat his university held for academic deans. The two-day retreat was held off campus at a posh resort as a paean to soothe the poor attendees' brows. Retreats can be good. Retreats can be productive. Industry uses retreats all the time to make certain that everyone is on the same page as far as operations and strategic plans go. Retreats are especially useful for leveling the performance playing field—for communicating to the laggards that they better get busy or seek employment elsewhere.

Following is the agenda of activities taking the majority of his university's high-level administrators (i.e., president, provost, vice president, associate provosts, and deans) off duty for two entire days. The first morning was devoted to presentations by the president and provost on the institutional and higher education environment (four hours). After lunch each dean presented on what they were doing regarding external development (4.5 hours). Lunch, reception, and dinner added another 3.5 hours. The second day consisted entirely of informational sessions totaling up to ten hours when adding in lunch and a final social reception.

We could calculate the actual cost of this retreat if we wanted to make a number of assumptions, but it's really not necessary. This example is presented to drive home a very important point about opportunity costs and stewardship of the public trust. What did the retreat accomplish? According to my colleague, it communicated information, but not necessarily new information. No decisions were made. No tough issues involving difficult working relations among this group of administrators were resolved.

In the end the retreat used up a lot of time and wasted funds on conference rooms, meals, and beverages that could have been better spent elsewhere. But it is the abuse of time that should most capture our attention. When these academic administrators are busy in their retreat, they aren't out there raising funds (remember they were *talking about* raising funds, not doing it); they aren't grappling with tough resource questions; they aren't working with faculty to streamline degree programs or to assure learning outcomes; and they aren't making wise use of their time.

Economists like to ruminate about opportunity costs, the cost of forgone opportunities when your time and attention are directed elsewhere. When we waste resources in academic circles, particularly time, there is a distinct cost plus the loss of forgone opportunities. How many of those deans might have raised $5,000 (or more) if those twenty-two hours were actually spent meeting with potential donors? What sorts of tangible strategic directions in which the university would build excellence could the provost and president have defined in a joint meeting lasting half of those twenty-two hours? Unfortunately these lost opportunities seldom seem to cross the radar screen of academic administrators.

Externalizing Internal Problems

It's these little indicators that tend to add up to significant trouble as far as academia is concerned. If you have a cavalier attitude toward your time, then maybe, just maybe, you will carry this attitude over to where it really counts on fiscal matters. If the culture of an organization—any organization, whether university or not—reinforces a lackadaisical attitude toward resource management, then we shouldn't be surprised when suddenly nothing is important or sacred.

Stanley Fish, former dean of the College of Liberal Arts and Sciences at the University of Chicago, published an article in the *Chronicle of Higher Education* that examines the outfall from careless attitudes by university administration (Fish, 2004). Fish recounts a recent mystery novel published by Jonathan Kellerman. The hero of the series conducts an interview with a department chair of a small college. In this fictional account, the chair grouses about how she was recruited to this college with lavish promises of programmatic support. She turned her back on more prestigious institutions because of these promises. After landing on campus the new chair quickly discovers that the promises were made of sand.

Fish uses this example to convey how widespread deception is in academic circles. Even popular mystery novels are aware of the shortcoming and critical of how academia operates. Fish expresses particular concern for faculty and staff morale:

"Many academics teaching in public universities have now concluded that there is not much to hope for (at least in the way of support) and that the only thing they are going to see in the future is a further deterioration of conditions of scarcity that are already appalling."

Dean Fish's lament is understandable, particularly when viewed in the context that he signed a contract to take his college to a new level of academic distinction—a goal that is most improbable given funding trends. However, his concern relates to the inability of academic leaders (ostensibly those above him such as the provost, president, and trustees) to argue persuasively with politicians to fund the university's needs and the lack of private donations to make up the difference—that is, private funding to cover the loss of public funding. In short, the university development office and president are just not doing their jobs, or at least not doing them very effectively.

Too many academics and academic administrators see the problem of constrained resources as one of external funding. Either the state is not willing to fund higher education over other programs, or private individuals (such as alumni) and philanthropists of wealth have shifted their giving to causes other than universities. None of these parties understand the predicament within universities and the sorrowful toll it is taking on faculty and staff. Students are ultimately the losers as programs shrink and quality heads south.

When deaning and vice presidenting, I too endured and resolutely negotiated many years of deficit and zero-increase budgets. Thus, I can commiserate with Dean Fish because it is extremely depressing to watch strong programs begin to erode as an artifact of diminishing resources. But, as I watched inept fumbling by top administrators—people who were paid to provide the requisite enlightened leadership for grappling with the dilemma—I came away with a vastly different interpretation of reality than Dean Fish.

My wake-up call came one cloud-covered winter day as I sat in a conference room of the central administrative building. I wrangled one of the perfect seats looking out on stately blue spruce trees and the gnarly skeletons of cottonwoods. Bruise-colored clouds flew by overhead while cold sunny rays bounced back into the meeting room. Outside it was frigid, but the tableau unfolding before my eyes was stunning. Too bad the meeting wasn't going to reach this pinnacle.

During the two-hour session our provost asked the assembled deans for their ideas about how to address the funding problems confronting the university. After almost five years of a stable budget and two years of exploding freshman admissions, every school and college was feeling the pinch. Thus commenced the gripe-and-moan session about how each school was destitute. There was no way we could continue under the present circumstances. Relief was needed in a big way if the university was expected to survive. The best professors were already departing. Needless to say, it was an exceptionally long two hours as my colleagues despaired about their respective academic units and how academic quality would suffer if the trend continued another minute.

We did manage to put together a list of ideas about resolving the funding problems facing this august institution:

- Increase undergraduate enrollments (to increase state funding)
- Increase graduate enrollments (to increase state funding)
- Increase development office efforts to raise donations
- Push the state to redefine formula funding to favor four-year colleges
- Increase tuition and fees 30 percent

With each suggestion my discomfort grew.

I kept my head down in an attempt to be called on last because I wanted to hear what the others had to say. Almost from the beginning I charted a single predominant theme that was very disturbing—each dean essentially echoed Dean Fish's lament. *We simply need an infusion of funds.*

Variants of this theme were shared as we went around the table. We've cut to the bone and there are no more slack resources to trim.

Students are facing hefty tuition increases because the state budget is depleted. Alumni giving is falling precipitously. Our best faculty members are looking elsewhere because they haven't had a raise in too many years. The president and regents should be lobbying the legislature on our behalf. Even if there was a budget increase of 10 to 15 percent, the damage cannot be undone. Collectively heads nodded with each assertion. Brows furrowed and eyebrows were raised with each more compelling argument.

I sat there stunned. They didn't get it. They just didn't get it. Here they were whining about the lack of raise money for two years when the rest of society was grappling with reduction-in-force programs—massive layoffs. How many of those people without jobs would care because some poor professors didn't have a raise in two years? At least the professors had jobs. Good paying jobs for only nine months' work. Businesses were hurting badly in the recession and having a difficult time making payroll; they were struggling to keep from going under. They really knew what cutting to the bone meant. Plus it was their livelihood, their capital, at risk.

Time was up. I would be called on next. What could I say? If I was true to my academic unit, then I should go along and cry big crocodile tears about how our enrollments had gone up steadily the last five years (unlike other colleges) and how we were beginning to slip under accreditation standards for faculty coverage. But I couldn't bring myself to continue blowing smoke, to tell a lie about how I really felt. It was time to share a minority opinion.

My message was not well received. As I looked around the table, sweet virtuous smiles gradually slipped off their faces. The provost looked like I had just informed them that the governor was closing the university next week. Brows began to crease. Several suddenly found pages on the tabletop far more interesting then the discussion. They tried to avoid eye contact with each other. Those sitting next to me gradually rolled their chairs away, grasping desperately for space, for distance from the heretic sitting next to them.

I tried to keep it short and sweet. We could not anticipate an increase in revenues. In fact, the probabilities favored a decreased budget. *We needed to control costs and reallocate resources internally while simultaneously raising productivity.*

My colleagues could only think in terms of their existing budgets plus an increment—2 percent, 5 percent, whatever. They assumed that their existing budget and resources were already being put to the highest and best use. Yet there had been no systematic, comprehensive analysis of budgets, resource productivity, or outcomes assessment by any academic unit, nor by the university as a whole. The deans and provost simply went with the premise that they could make no cuts, that reallocation was unthinkable, and that the only way out of the predicament was to receive more funding.

I tired to briefly explain that the university was finally being asked to do what families had already done. Families were struggling to cope. Family incomes had leveled or were cut drastically as people lost jobs or suffered salary/wage reductions. Families were being forced to live on less. In this case, families had to look at their expenditures and make decisions about what they would live without, or they had to increase their productivity by taking on another job—another source of income. They had a budget, and they had to live with it. No one was there to bail them out—not the legislature, not the alumni, not the state taxpayer.

Businesses had gone through the same phenomenon and internal searching. Resources they employed were reduced. Remaining resources—employees—were called on to be more productive. Staffs were trimmed to skeletal levels. Survivors were asked to do the job that many more used to do or to seek employment elsewhere. Everyone was being stretched, asked to do more with less. Businesses were devoting fanatical attention to measuring productivity *and* quality. Global competition was forcing businesses to be much more efficient and to achieve this efficiency now or go bankrupt.

Yes, universities are finally facing the same pressures that the public and businesses have already stared in the ugly face. It is now our turn to pay the piper, to tighten the belt, and to demonstrate that we are effective stewards of the resources entrusted to us. There is no magic solution, no silver bullet, for the problems facing universities. *We have to seek solutions internally.*

The provost glanced at the clock and turned to the executive assistant. "Yes, we are almost out of time [saved by the bell]. This had been a hugely important discussion and we will continue looking for ways to resolve the dilemma. If we think of any other approaches, please email me with your ideas. Thanks for the meaningful input."

As we pushed back from the conference table and my colleagues hurriedly tried to avoid an acknowledging glance or dangerous word or two, I realized that I had taken them far beyond their comfort level. They didn't want to confront faculty and staff about their productivity. They didn't want to ask faculty to teach more students or more sections. That isn't how deans continue to remain dean. If the legislature could just give us a 3 percent increase, everything would be alright for one more year. Or even 2 percent—that would be enough. Reallocation? Cut costs? Raise productivity? You've got to be kidding. That's not my job.

The implications of the preceding vignette for saving higher education are far-reaching. Until universities better manage the resources they possess, they won't be receiving much sympathy from the public. Universities must demonstrate that they are first achieving the highest and best use of resources before the public will shower them with additional funding. Once credibility has been achieved in how existing resources are being managed effectively, then taxpayer ears will begin to open concerning wailing pleas about additional funding.

Whether universities like it or not, external pressures for intelligent management of resources are on the rise. Fiscal thri-val (not just survival, but thrive-ability) plans for the immediate future must necessarily be based on several key premises:

- Public funding will continue to be constrained.
- Tuition rates cannot be increased dramatically.
- Corporate, foundation, and governmental research funding will be increasingly difficult to obtain.

This is a fairly glum forecast, and it implies that traditional models for sustaining higher education financing are basically bankrupt.

Despite such constraints there is still room for optimism if we think robustly about how to achieve higher and better uses of existing resources while strategizing for new sources of revenue. Let's consider the case of most medium-to-large public universities. Key strategy elements for thriving in the future include:

1. Institute rigorous annual programmatic evaluation and assessment to identify programs that need to be retired as well as those that should be grown. Reallocate resources

from programs that are phased out. Generate resources internally to enrich distinctive programs. This implies that a university will become less a broad public good and more focused on distinctiveness. Prune the curriculum to save valuable resources. Reduce the menu of small specialty classes (in areas that are not selected to be grown for distinctiveness) by force of fiscal prudence.

2. Focus on a narrow range of superior-performing academic programs after building a strong core curriculum to achieve the highest and best use of resources and funds. Do not try to be everything to everybody. Establish a brand on the basis of a strong general education with distinctive value-added characteristics through selective specializations and majors.

3. Adopt a best value strategy—deliver high quality education at a modest price. This will ensure a steady stream of high-quality students that capitalizes on maximizing available state funding.

4. Generate new revenue streams through intellectual property commercialization, high-demand boutique programs (phased in and out depending on demand and performance), and alternative delivery to niche markets (especially foreign markets).

5. Develop meaningful linkages with international universities to broaden market reach and to globalize home campus experience. Increasingly, foreign students will seek to obtain a U.S. college experience. Astute universities will enable highly qualified and fiscally capable foreign students to access their programs (e.g., dividing class time between home country and main campus). The ideal model will be a lean full-service Division I university with vibrant athletics, an attractive community social scene, and high quality of life.

6. Rigorously cultivate the most senior alumni through planned giving to create a steady flow of mega-gifts.

7. Integrate pre-alumni (i.e., students) and young alumni within an electronic-based social fabric/network to establish giving traditions and reinforce value-added relations. Mimic the best Ivy League schools in pre-graduation cultivation while using contemporary electronic approaches.

8. Accentuate lifelong education and career development (instead of jobs). Invest in strong career planning and placement and developing deep associations with employers—this will ensure a steady stream of students (attracted by great jobs) combined with lucrative corporate support (corporations that use a university's talent/ graduates should pay to access this talent).

9. Encourage all undergraduates to earn an entrepreneurship minor. This will motivate them to think more carefully about how they will ultimately use their degree and in the process possibly achieve greater professional success. Greater career success will spell larger alumni donations in the long run.

The preceding plan has applicability to about 60 to 70 percent of all institutions. Extremely large and/or well-endowed universities (private and public) and extremely small and/or highly niche-focused universities will necessarily adopt alternative strategies. For the majority of public universities there is more promise in right-sizing—an in-between size of 20,000 to 30,000 students—rather than in being too large or too small.

Although the strategy spelled out above is relatively parsimonious, its elegant simplicity belies an elevated degree of difficulty in execution (generally due to well-ingrained faculty cultures). Nonetheless the strategy integrates both internal and external tactics to increase funds while promoting the highest and best use of resources.

INTERNAL STRATEGIES TO ACHIEVE HIGHEST AND BEST RESOURCE USE

How does a university actually go about the day-to-day process of achieving the highest and best use of resources? Many roads appear to lead to this goal, but few will choose the narrow, rocky path that's required. The secret is to create a culture that continually assesses how resources are being invested while routinely ascertaining the outcomes associated with those investments. Essentially this means adopting more of a corporate model for academic administration, a prescription that is a very bitter pill for academics to swallow.

Applying rigorous business concepts is one thing, but inculcating a culture that is comfortable with these ideas, that stands behind inevitable change associated with assessment and reallocation, is quite another. This is a daunting challenge because academic administration has been so sloppy in demonstrating that resources are put to good use (much less the highest and best use). One thing is certain, headway will never be made unless all of the top administrative team—regents, president, provost, deans, and department heads—are on the same page.

If you treat one—just one—department or college differently than another, your initiative will come unglued. By this I mean preferential treatment that allows a unit to live down to a standard the rest have to exceed. For example, if all departments in the college of arts and sciences submit a budget that is based on 80 percent of the preceding year's budget and geology only has to submit a budget that is at the 90 percent level because it has been building back its faculty, the process has been corrupted.

There is too much information sharing to allow preferential treatment. Once the word slips out—and it will, because academic tongues love to wag—the dean will be facing incensed department chairs that begin to fudge analyses and documentation of results. Academics are terribly brilliant; they will find ways to play games that minimize their unit's budget impact. This is exactly what you do not want to motivate.

The goal is to inculcate an honest appraisal of resource expenditures and returns from those expenditures. At the same time, we *do* want differential treatment but only after transparent documentation and analysis of results. That's the only way that one chair will buy into another department receiving a bigger budget increase. When incontrovertible proof exists that a department has taken resources and produced more, or when a department is already producing more and needs additional funds to keep growing, these are the situations in which differential treatment becomes widely accepted, defensible, and culturally acceptable.

Remember, it only takes one violation for the process to crumble. It's far more effective to share information and rationales regarding why differential treatment will occur than to let speculation run rampant in the halls. Both provosts and deans will try to avoid transparency. They hate to make differential decisions because it means potentially creating enemies. But, if we are going to save higher education we—they— have no choice. The dirty deed must be done.

Having been in charge of multimillion-dollar budgets for many years at a variety of institutions I will admit that not every resource dollar under my control was producing a maximum return on investment. Why was I somewhat negligent in achieving maximum return on resources invested? *No overarching university climate encouraged such behavior.* In fact, the incentives were all in the wrong direction. Under a current-budget-plus-a-percentage-increase model, there were only disincentives to act as a good steward. There certainly were no incentives to confront department chairs about their resource mismanagement. There was no orchestrated protection from potential litigation due to cutting faculty or staff positions (in fact just the opposite climate existed; administrators who took a tough stand had to first prove their innocence).

Resource assessment and reallocation invariably imply that some faculty and staff will be terminated to transfer funds to another academic unit or to reassign funds within a college or department. The university as a whole (or the state) might have to adopt a policy of financial exigency to protect itself from potentially harmful litigation. If a department chair or dean is unable to terminate a faculty or staff member because of potential legal liability, then reallocation is going to be virtually impossible.

Theoretically the highest and best use of resources should be accompanied by zero-base budgeting. Under this approach every resource is scrutinized every year for possible reallocation. This approach will quickly chase away the mentality that the base budget is fixed and next year's budget will represent an increment added on to that base. This mentality of a fixed-base budget is doing serious harm to academia. It perpetuates the status quo and acts against innovation within units. The incentive is to keep things as they have been the previous year.

Could those resources be made more productive? How? What changes are needed to instill change? How about the consolidation of resources or the refocusing of resources? Has there been a change in mission, strategy, or objectives that suggest altering how resources are allocated? These questions are never answered under a current-budget-plus-percentage-increase mentality. I submit that it is precisely these questions that academia must answer, and answer soundly, before it can lay claim to effective resource management.

Not too surprisingly, this is the sort of public-sector mindset that is linked to academic tenure. Faculty members often behave as if they have permanent employment. They extrapolate this into thinking that their college will always need *at least* the existing number of faculty positions their academic unit possesses. Staff members tend to be treated in the same forgiving manner; that is, the unit will always need those that currently work at the college plus more. The college can't do with less; it actually needs more. Therefore there is no reason to question how many people the unit has, what theses staff members are doing, or what they produce. In short, the university becomes a form of social employment program.

To implement a system of zero-base budgeting centered on rigorous strategic planning, top leaders—regents, presidents, provosts, faculty senate presidents, and faculty senators—will have to make tough calls. In particular, strategic plans incorporating specific statements about vision, mission, objectives, and strategies for achieving the plan are essential as a guideline for decision-making. Top leaders will have to initiate and reinforce systematic, comprehensive performance analysis. They will have to make tough calls on where resources will be reallocated and which units stand to lose because of these decisions.

It's precisely this hard work, rigorous analysis, and tough decision-making that has encouraged top administration in many universities to not take a hard line. But, increasingly, state-supported higher education is being forced to undergo this sort of cleansing introspection. Force of circumstance tends to be the driving rationale for adopting business-centered practices. For others without these driving forces, a mentality prevails that if you can avoid it, do so.

Consequently, it may be easier for universities to implement something along the lines of 80 percent base budgeting. By focusing on 20 percent of vulnerable resources, it may be possible to avoid some of the strife associate with across the board exposure to budget review. Additionally, a 20 percent analysis is more achievable from an applications standpoint. But let's be honest about the matter. Even with a 20 percent approach, there will extraordinary turmoil and political activity. The outcry will be most impressive. That's why university leaders need to stand behind each other.

To ease into an 80 percent budgeting scenario, a number of approaches are feasible. Each unit might prepare an 80 percent budget and demonstrate how that budget is consistent with, and simultaneously conflicts with, its strategic plan. Explanations should emphasize the positive and negative impacts from an 80 percent budget. Units could present plans for how they might reallocate the 20 percent if they are allowed to retain the funds. The president, provost, committee of vice presidents, or some such decision-making body can decide who retains and who relinquishes funds (from 1 to 20 percent). Alternatively, the provost might indicate a target of give-back funding before relying on deans to make the call for their units about funding reallocations.

Again, it cannot be emphasized strongly enough that consistency, integrity, transparency, analysis, and rigor accompany all efforts at budget reallocation. Without a systematic and comprehensive process, the prospects for serious turmoil are too high. The goal is to evolve higher education not create a self-destructing revolution.

Budgeting is only one way to steer higher education toward a new mindset and a new operating reality. The academic community must rely on these technical assists to build a new philosophy about respect for resources. Wise management of funding and careful attention to detail in expending resources are not difficult concepts for intelligent academics to grasp.

A CALL TO ACTION FOR FACULTY

Academics find the corporatization of academia revolting, yet they do very little to prevent the spread of these ideas. If they (we) encouraged their department chairs and deans to ask the question, "Is this the highest and best use of this resource?" on a more frequent basis, perhaps we would see less external pressure for the adoption of business practices within our ivy-covered walls. But faculty members usually fail to rise to the occasion. They continue to stick their heads in the sand hoping it will all go away. Recognizing that progress has been slow to come to academia, that they are the last bastion of bureaucratic inefficiency, their mythical dream is that things will remain just as they always have been and that a return to the good old times is shortly over the next horizon.

Here is the rub and the call to action for faculty. What if instead of waiting for academic administrators to tell them how it's going to be done, the faculty became a genesis for a new academic environment? What would happen if faculty took the initiative to set things right in higher education, to make certain that every resource attains its highest and best use? Instead of sitting around waiting for someone else to solve our problems, what if faculty, the educated, took responsibility for the mess? What would happen if they rose to the occasion?

Imagine how strong our higher education system might become if the dog wagged its tail instead of waiting for the tail to wag the dog. The faculty is the most enduring part of any university. Collectively, faculty members can establish a more enlightened approach to university administration and to stewardship of public resources. They can press for innovations in how the university is operated. They can argue persuasively for more enlightened management of resources. Faculty members have everything to gain from such advocacy. Research and teaching can be greatly enhanced when resources are put to better use.

The only thing preventing faculty from adopting a leadership approach is an excessive comfort level. They have had things too good for too long. Why bother to change? Well, the answer is quite simple. If faculty members don't take some time out from their research and teaching to lead and participate in the constructive evolution of higher education, they will discover that the public (via legislators), regents, presidents, and provosts will tell them how their reality is going to change. And faculty members are not going to like the scenarios staring them in the face.

Unless university faculties assume leadership for ensuring the highest and best use of resources at their campuses, a new, vastly changed world of higher education will evolve. Gone will be the perquisites. Ruthlessly cold, hard assessments of resource expenditures will sweep over campuses. The old academic life will evaporate, replaced by rigorous business models that give no quarter to research or teaching that fail to add value to students' education.

Is this the future academics want? Is this the legacy that the professorate will leave to the next generation of bright young minds entering our doctoral programs? It doesn't have to be this way. I hope that it doesn't come to this. It simply is a matter of doggedly advocating sanity in how we put resources to their highest and best use.

Chapter 5

ALIGNING INCENTIVES WITH REALITY

L
ong before the notion of an inalienable right to free speech, people had to be fairly circumspect about what they expressed. If someone espoused a view that was contrary to a current regime's thinking, the price paid could be fairly draconian, such as death. In academia, this prospect was quite problematic for professors who wanted to delve into the many complex and often emotional dimensions of leading sensitive topics. Medieval universities were fundamentally about archiving knowledge, transmitting it to students, and, with proper discretion, critically analyzing ideas. The ability to openly challenge conventional wisdom or to explore and publicly advocate concepts not in vogue was constrained. Academicians could not contribute as meaningfully as they might wish to the evolution of knowledge. Lacking constitutional protections of free speech, university professors faced significant risk to livelihood and health even in the mundane execution of their daily responsibilities.

Clearly the peril of speaking out had to be mitigated to encourage the vibrant expression of new ideas and to advance knowledge across the academic disciplines. Protection of professorial free speech prerogatives was critical to enable open, lively discussions in lecture halls and classrooms. Ensuring continued employment, despite one's academic opinions, was one means that universities could use to protect faculty and at the same time cultivate a fertile learning environment essential to intellectual discovery.

Enter the revered institution known as tenure.

Walter P. Metzger prepared an illuminating report on the history of tenure for the Commission on Academic Tenure in Higher Education (1973). He notes that:

> Tenure in magisterial universities was not an attribute of occupancy of office, with set emoluments and prescribed functions, but an attribute of admission to a *corpus*, possessed

of a legal personality and (in part through delegation, in part through usurpation) of considerable governmental power, of a kind of mini-sovereignty. Admission to this body was accomplished not through a contract of employment but through the crossing of certain qualificatory thresholds—the earning of degrees, the exhibition of certain prowesses, the acquisition of a license—over which the masters took command. Continuation as a member depended not on the performance of specific duties . . . but on adherence to collegial comities. And expulsion from this body could be directly affected not by an outside agency but only by the body itself.

The essence of Metzger's point is that during medieval times, tenure granted admission to a collegial body of scholars. Subsequently in the mid-eighteenth century (in America), lay control of universities prevailed over clerical overseers and church mandates. Tenure became directly linked with specific institutions instead of the profession (Metzger, 1973). At this point universities began defining policies regarding tenure rights and privileges.

Unbridled thinking, passionate discourse, and public proclamations of seemingly heretical ideas carried the risk of external retaliation (Brubacher & Rudy, 1997). Influential people of means, beleaguered politicians, and offended royalty could be very persuasive when pressuring university masters, dons, chancellors, and trustees to quell what they saw as the gibberish ideas advocated by faculty members. In the face of this possible retaliation, it is not clear how many professors took the high road by not compromising either their lectures or dissemination of ideas. How many suffered the ignominy of losing a coveted faculty position because of what they believed, what they vehemently espoused and thought? From this humble but tumultuous background sprang tenure.

Michael Scriven is an eminent philosopher with degrees in mathematics and mathematical logic and a doctorate in philosophy from Oxford. He has been associated with many distinguished universities including the University of Auckland in New Zealand, Claremont Graduate School, and Western Michigan University. Don't let these impressive credentials sour your opinion of Dr. Scriven; he is one of academia's free thinkers who have wrestled with the thorny problems of evaluation.

Almost by dint of his many academic appointments, Dr. Scriven is suitably qualified to comment on that sacred cow known as academic tenure. He has opined that "[t]he juvenile sea squirt wanders through the ocean searching for a suitable rock or hunk of coral to cling to and make a home for its life. When it finds its spot and takes root, it doesn't need its brain anymore, so it eats it. It's rather like getting tenure." Judging by the number of times this quotation has been cited, a sizeable number of people couldn't agree more about academia's most infamous perquisite.

In my opinion, granting tenure is perhaps the single most important factor that has damaged the sustainability of a vibrant intellectual climate in modern higher education. Legions of otherwise vastly capable university faculty have been sullied by granting tenure.

What is this thing called tenure, and how is it bestowed? Most people outside the ivory tower only recognize that tenure means someone has a permanent job, although technically that isn't quite correct. Even those who should be in the know—regents, trustees, and other lay leaders (such as foundation and advisory board members)—seem perplexed about tenure. They know that it exists. They know that tenure makes faculty members relatively immune to termination and consequently a formidable challenge for academic administrators. They know that tenure must be earned, but they don't have a clue about the processes that ultimately lead to a tenure decision. In view of this confusion it's appropriate to spend a few minutes on a tenure primer (AAUP, 1915; AAUP, 1940).

THE TENURE PROCESS

Universities normally hire new faculty in one of two ways: tenure track faculty (those aspiring to receive tenure) and supporting faculty (those that do not aspire to receive tenure). Typically tenure track faculty members have earned what is known as a "terminal degree," the highest educational degree in a field. In most cases a terminal degree implies a doctorate, but it is essential to recognize that some fields, such as architecture, do not have doctoral degrees. Supporting faculty may also have earned a terminal degree, but due to professional and personal circumstances, they are not aspiring to earn tenure.

A newly hired tenure-track faculty member is given a certain time period—often six years—in which to earn tenure. These faculty members generally must demonstrate the ability to attain distinguished performance in teaching and research (with satisfactory service), and the promise to continue performing at high levels. Universities whose mission is teaching tend to emphasize instructional excellence and dissemination of instructional scholarship as tenure criteria. Research-oriented institutions emphasize the ability to publish research in leading academic journals and the ability to fund research independently while generally downplaying teaching expectations. Universities emphasizing a blend of teaching and research give substantial weight to both performance areas while expecting distinction in one.

As the preceding explanation suggests, there is a great deal of latitude in defining what it takes to earn tenure. What qualifies in one department, college, or university may not fly in another. Missions vary among academic units and within disciplines (and sub-disciplines) further confusing the issue. Compounding the problem is assessment of the intellectual products and teaching performance. There is no single defined standard of what constitutes high quality teaching or research. For example, some would argue that publication in a field's leading journals is the standard for high quality. Yet a seminal contribution to a narrow field published in a relatively obscure journal (but the top journal in that sub-discipline) may be seen as superior to a record with numerous top-level journal publications spread over several disciplines (i.e., more widely read journals that are not necessarily the top journal in the sub-discipline).

In the final analysis, enormous judgment comes into play when determining whether a candidate merits tenure. The situation is made more complex by the many faculty members who render their opinions regarding each candidate's record. Typically faculty within an academic department submit an opinion on a candidate's tenure to the department chair, who forwards a recommendation to the dean along with opinions rendered by external leaders in the field. The dean may seek counsel from faculty in the college outside the candidate's academic department before submitting a recommendation to the provost. In turn, the provost makes a recommendation to the president and thence to the regents or trustees.

Tenure candidates generally spend six years trying to achieve what it takes to earn tenure; that is, the performance that is expected from them in teaching, research, and service. They have labored to meet these expectations while knowing that ambiguous standards can change depending on who is in control. They have had to negotiate sensitive faculty politics while being very careful not to offend or step on the toes of senior faculty. In short, junior faculty members are expected to grovel professionally, to keep their mouths shut, and to produce expected performance or risk not earning tenure.

Alas the best intentions and research programs invariably encounter difficulties. A new faculty member may be swamped with course preparations because her or his doctoral institution required minimal doctoral teaching. This constrains the ability to complete research and disseminate findings. Or a brilliant piece of scholarly work may be given to eccentric external reviewers associated with the field's leading journal. They may request one or more rounds of revisions only to reject the manuscript after the paper has been in the review process for several years. Other scholars may have grand success in publishing, but they fail to hit it off with students due to language differences, learning expectations, teaching style, and similar confounding factors. In short, there are plenty of dead ends waiting for those who try to negotiate tenure territory.

POST-TENURE TRANSFORMATIONS

It should come as little surprise that after six years of indentured service (not counting the three to five—or more—years indentured labor as a doctoral student) those faculty who earn tenure typically tend to let down for a couple of years. This is obviously a generalization, and many professors continue along as they have before earning tenure. Nonetheless, in my experience numerous faculty members—even the very best— have a propensity to embrace tenure and to cut back (however briefly) on their performance. They may have earned a one semester sabbatical, which they infer is a just reward for jumping through all of the hoops along the way. The post-tenure decision period is very critical because it is not surprising to see some unfortunate transformations.

Candidates who have been squashed by senior faculty and doctoral mentors tend to come out of their shells in brash new ways. They may be quite vociferous about their opinions. Tenure gives free speech back to them, and they exercise it with a vengeance in the hallways, in meetings, and in the community. Some become very involved and quite skillful (because they have learned from experts over the years) in the politics of their department and college. Others who have marginal teaching or research records may take an extended vacation; they no longer invest as diligently in teaching or research because they never really liked teaching or research, or they never really had the capacity. They only did what was needed to attain tenure.

Given brutal doctoral apprenticeships, it is understandable why faculty members tend to become cantankerous and opinionated and act like prima donnas after earning tenure. Most people outside universities don't realize the number of milestones faculty must attain or the length of time required when earning tenure. The public only understands that faculty are bestowed an unbelievable perk—guaranteed employment. However, this is an overly generous interpretation of reality.

TENURE PERQUISITES

Most universities do not guarantee tenured faculty members a job. As long as a university has funds to operate, tenured faculty members have earned a right to expect employment and renewal of their faculty contract. Normally only in the case of a budget exigency (or commission of a felonious crime or reprehensible moral act) can universities terminate tenured faculty without the likely prospect of successful opposing litigation.

University leaders recognize that when you start cutting away sections of the tenured faculty you embark on a very slippery slope that ultimately descends more quickly toward collapse. It takes years—decades—to build strong faculties. Without a distinguished faculty, a university has very little. Even a superb football team can only compensate temporarily for a mediocre faculty because the tenured faculty is the enduring core of a university. Each semester new students and administrators—football players and teams, provosts, presidents, and regents—come and go, yet it is the tenured faculty that remains when all is said and done.

TENURE'S DOWNSIDE

If tenured faculty members are so precious, then why is tenure so bad? The primary shortcoming of tenure is its tendency to communicate the wrong incentives. Some faculty feel cozily protected from retaliation for almost any sort of indefensible behavior, ludicrous opinion, or inane meddling on their part. Others think that they can coast along in their work, having made the supreme effort to achieve tenure. They pontificate that student evaluations of their teaching are patently biased and only reflect opinions about entertainment capacity. They will argue that leading journals in their field don't know great research when they see it, or they are run by a bunch of dilettantes, so why bother submitting manuscripts in the first place?

To illustrate just how bad behavior can be under tenure, consider the college that was conducting a search for a new dean. As part of the process, a slate of four finalists was brought to campus for lengthy interviews. In the course of their visits, each candidate met in an open forum with faculty to exchange views and ascertain fit. One aspiring candidate opened the floor for questions. A tenured full professor asked an innocuous question about research. The candidate, trying to create a friendly climate and conversation, had been asking each faculty member who raised a question to share their name in creating a bit of friendliness.

The tenured full professor replied, "I don't need to tell you my name. Just answer the question. You're not the FBI. Just answer the question. You're not the FBI." What better way to draw attention to yourself than to behave in this manner. You can be certain that the candidate found out who that faculty member was after the meeting took place. But that's not the point.

What organization would tolerate this sort of behavior from an employee? This outburst violated the most fundamental expectation of common human decency by an educated professional. In some firms the offending employee wouldn't even make it back to her or his office, and justifiably so. Security would be waiting at the conference room door, ready to escort the former employee out the back door. Exceptional organizations don't have room for this sort of sick antic by employees. But in a system that supports tenure, such criminals are difficult to get rid of. Is this the enlightened behavior taxpayers expect when they are paying this professor's handsome salary? It was simply rudely infantile behavior stimulated in part by tenure and highly reflective of the individual's character.

For the vast majority of faculty, tenure doesn't motivate sudden shifts in professional or personal behavior. Tenure doesn't encourage them to be vocally negative or politically active to the detriment of their academic unit. But there is an insidious reality for *some* faculty members; tenure diminishes, or in extremes takes away, the drive to achieve. This disincentive may not be highly apparent until looking over records that span years.

For faculty members who are susceptible to clinging to tenure's coattails, the fall-off in performance is measurable. Fewer scholarly papers will be presented at leading academic meetings. Articles are submitted and published in lower-level academic or professional journals. Less effort is made to review manuscripts for journals or conferences. Class lectures remain stale and rooted in the past. Testing falls into a predictable malaise, and grades become inflated as faculty members grow weary of fighting to maintain standards.

In any other employment setting these sorts of behavioral changes are dealt with much more effectively. Low or no raises are given. Demotions and terminations occur. An enterprise approach prevails. Failure to support organizational initiatives, mission and goals, or policies is met head-on. Confrontation is more likely to happen and with it penalties for poor performance or substandard conduct. Perhaps more than anything else, the specter of losing one's job is a sufficient deterrent to acting like an idiot, shirking job responsibilities, or coasting along on other's coattails.

ANNUAL REVIEWS AND TENURE

On the surface two processes exist—annual performance reviews and post-tenure review—that in theory ought to keep faculty honest as far as incentives surrounding tenure. First is the annual performance review—evaluation of performance in anticipation of salary increases. Department chairs and deans will frequently work diligently to develop rigorous annual performance reviews. Their thinking goes something like this: If annual performance is carefully reviewed and documented, then there is a basis for differentiating the types of rewards faculty receive, there is a written record of needed improvements that's useful when planning for faculty development, and there is sufficient documentation to pursue revocation of tenure if performance remains substandard.

Unfortunately several factors militate against meaningful performance reviews. Foremost are the funding prospects for salary increases to public employees in higher education. Take 2003 as an example. In that year, only three states reported non-deficit budgets; that is, only three states appeared to have the wherewithal to allocate salary increases to public employees in higher education. As it turned out, some states encouraged tuition increases in 2003 to fund salary increases and others allowed universities to cannibalize vacant positions to fund salary increases. The point is that funding for state employee salary increases had been marginal. Faculty members know this and may respond accordingly by lowering their effort and output.

In the last decade of vagaries surrounding state budgets, it has been common for faculty to receive no raises, or very modest raises, or a combination of both. No matter how much time a department chair invests in assessing performance and in encouraging faculty to perform better, reality reaches home in the actual limited amount of money to distribute in annual raises. Inevitably after only one year of no raise money, pressures the following year are overwhelming on academic administrators to make certain everyone receives a healthy slug of cost-of-living adjustment regardless of performance. Combine several years where no or little increase has been allocated and pressures mount even further.

For all of their idealism and pontifications about how other aspects of life are more important than money, in the end faculty tend to be like most people. They expect a certain standard of living. They expect hard work to be rewarded. And they almost universally view their performance as being more than satisfactory even when it isn't.

All a department chairman has to do is simply raise a question about teaching effectiveness or call into question the strength of a journal to understand faculty sensitivity to performance assessments. Granted, a large part of faculty reaction is ego driven, but an equally significant portion of their reaction relates to how much money they will earn in the future.

Department chairs who review performance and dish out the raises face daunting peer pressure to tread lightly on subpar performance. Department chairs typically hold their position for four years before returning to the faculty ranks. They intuitively understand that should they make enemies it could come back to haunt them in very significant ways in the future. Consequently, there is a tendency to level raises by distributing them equally across the board.

Compounding this problem is the ambiguity of performance assessment. Faculty members strive to achieve outcomes in three areas—teaching, research, and service. The type of activities and outcomes and measurements used to assess performance within each of these areas are far from uniform. The result is a proverbial dilemma of equating apples, oranges, and watermelons. Consequently, assessment becomes even more complex when the overall performance portfolio for any faculty member is compared to other faculty.

If the preceding shortcomings in annual performance reviews aren't sufficient to jeopardize fair and impartial evaluations, another problem rears its ugly head. Department chairs have a notorious tendency to turn over. They receive limited additional salary for a complicated and high-stress job, they have to spend many more hours on campus instead of sequestered doing research, and they have to fight with their friends. Every time turnover occurs within a department, it threatens the consistency of standards and the manner in which they are applied. The same impact occurs from department chair turnover at the college level. There is a failure to apply consistent standards and to build institutional memory about how a faculty member's performance has been managed.

Methodological problems associated with annual performance reviews ultimately come home to roost in terms of tenure. To remove tenure when a faculty member is performing below the standard expected for her or his rank, clear and unambiguous evidence must exist that he or she was informed about the specific performance deficiencies. Sounds simple enough, but given turnover in faculty administrators (i.e., department chairs and deans), a pattern of very modest to no raises, and the reluctance of administrators to be harsh on their colleagues, it is easy to understand why many faculty members receive non-critical performance reviews each year.

POST-TENURE REVIEWS

A second process (in addition to annual performance reviews) has been instilled in many universities as a means to keep tenured faculty honest. Post-tenure review is a euphemism used to suggest that universities are willing to police their very own. In fact, most tenure review processes have limited bite and exist as only a paean to regents, trustees, and legislators. Colleagues really have no intention of getting rid of a tenured colleague because it would set a precedent that ultimately could come back to bite them personally. Provosts and presidents don't want sticky, litigious issues going before their regents and trustees because it may reflect badly on their performance. As a result, post-tenure review is a great idea in concept, but many times it's worthless in terms of practical value.

Post-tenure review processes are commonly triggered by annual reviews. For example, a faculty member who receives two deficient annual reviews may inadvertently launch the post-tenure review process. After the second deficient review, the department chair and senior faculty undertake a more in-depth review. Depending on their findings, and with concurrence of the affected party, they devise a plan for remediation. Typically the faculty member then has two to three years to achieve this plan.

If performance at the conclusion of this period is still lacking, *the department* usually must decide whether to press for tenure revocation. Remember that universities rely on collegial governance. Remember that in the course of a five-year period, a faculty member can virtually count on having at least two different deans and department chairs. Remember that performance assessment is ambiguous and squishy due to a dearth of defensible measures and lack of comparability among teaching, research, and service products. Given these preconditions, what relatively new department chair or dean wants to invest much of their time with lawyers either in or out of court trying to justify why they recommended that tenure be withdrawn?

The prospects for post-tenure review may not be as dismal as surface impressions suggest. Deans and department chairs who maintain rigor during annual reviews and distribution of salary increases (and other remuneration) can get the job done without revoking tenure. The only problem is that this strategy takes years to play out—a length of time that those in the private sector simply find unacceptable.

Consider the case of a faculty member who was a marginal pass for tenure. The professor in question barely had sufficient research publications to merit a claim of promise of distinction—the minimum to merit granting of tenure. It was a tough call for the dean, especially because the department chair was unwilling to characterize research performance as less than excellent. The faculty member in question had provided evidence of satisfactory teaching, although there were occasional classes over the preceding six years in which unsatisfactory ratings surfaced. The correct call appeared to be one of giving this faculty member the benefit of the doubt.

How did the newly tenured faculty member respond? First, he immediately shut down his research productivity. He virtually stopped working on new manuscript drafts or participating in academic societies. Second, his teaching scores plummeted. In fact, student comments roundly criticized the professor for his arrogant, condescending attitude. He remained aloof, unwilling to assist students in learning course material, and critical of the quality of students and their study habits.

Before long the professor had accumulated two negative annual performance reviews. Fortunately over these two years the university in question did not receive any raises. In the third year, a new department chair arrived on the scene and undertook a more in depth review (as promulgated by university faculty policy). Department faculty rallied around their colleague and minimized the expectations for remediation. However, raise money was distributed, and the new department chair refused to award even a minimum salary increase (consistent with a cost-of-living adjustment) as recommended by the university.

The professor requested a leave without pay to spend a year earning a new masters degree. The leave was granted. At annual review time the professor did not submit any documentation of research productivity—an expectation that remained despite the leave without pay. The department chair again refused to award a salary increase. Finally, in the fifth year the department chair, department faculty, and dean indicated they would seek tenure revocation if the (fifth) annual review was not satisfactory. Four months later the faculty member in question resigned to take a position in industry.

Lessons from this example are numerous. First, tenure can create a sense of invincibility and nurture arrogance on the part of faculty, but tenure does not mean that perpetrators will avoid their deserved rewards. Second, faculty members tend to sympathize with each other, cover up deficient performance, and view substandard performance less critically than more objective third parties. Third, high turnover among department chairs, deans, and provosts enables substandard performers to avoid being held accountable. Fourth, a well-documented paper trail is difficult to establish given turnover among administrators; the documentation is vitally needed to defend against potential litigation.

There is another lesson from this vignette that deserves special consideration—the time required to oust the professor. Almost five years elapsed before the professor's position became vacant and available for a new faculty member. That's way too long. It is very difficult to build exceptional academic programs when you have to wait five years to see someone leave simply because they are misusing tenure to protect their rear end. It's this sort of tragic story that leaves taxpayers, regents, and legislators wagging their heads and vocalizing the need to terminate tenure.

IS THERE A COMPELLING NEED FOR TENURE?

A more fundamental question pertains to the need for tenure. Why do we even need tenure? This is question that not many faculty members take time to consider. If we go back to the origins of tenure when the right to free speech and expression of ideas were not guaranteed by a constitution, then perhaps some legitimacy accompanied academics' claims that they deserved special protection in the exchange of ideas. The very nature of discourse could sufficiently offend someone in a position of authority or power to the extent that they pressured the university to terminate faculty members.

The original rationale for awarding tenure just doesn't fly anymore. Free speech has been taken to such an extent by society that strong opinions and bizarre viewpoints held by college professors seem pretty tame in comparison. In fact, just the opposite can be argued—that we do not have enough free thinking and expression of radical ideas in universities. A benign homogeneity can creep within our disciplines. Those who step too far out of the box are summarily roped back in via very subtle pressures or shunned for their heretical thinking. Thoughts that are way off the scale tend to be ignored by the academy as a whole.

To be certain, there are still cases where professors offend the public, students, top administrator, regents and trustees, legislators, and others with their insensitive or ignorant statements. But only very rarely is someone condemned because they propose an idea that is counter to what everyone else thinks. It takes a very inflammatory statement, an immorally outrageous theory or proposition, or criminal behavior for people to react sufficiently that they call for the revocation of tenure. But, admittedly, these events still occur.

In the immediate days following September 11, 2001, a tenured professor issued a controversial remark in class condemning the actions of the United States and supporting the people of Iraq. A few students were blatantly offended by these statements. The matter continued to grow as the press played out the controversy. Regents received calls from the public demanding that the professor be summarily fired. The university's administrators found themselves in the uncomfortable position of defending the professor's right to free speech while simultaneously questioning the wisdom of the statement.

Almost everyone would agree that the statement was insensitive and ill-timed. Some would defend the professor because the event occurred in a history class in which such issues could legitimately be considered consistent with the curriculum. Others would characterize the statement and the professor as just stupid, raising the question of whether he should continue due to professional negligence.

In the end, the professor decided to retire. He was not fired. He did not have tenure revoked despite all of the blustery statements from legislators, regents and top administrators. He just retired. Although details will probably never be known, there is reason to suspect that the university and professor reached an amicable agreement regarding his retirement. It is highly likely that the university sweetened the pot by purchasing years of service or an annuity to get the job done. Such compensation would be given in exchange for tenure rights.

This example focuses on tenure's value, or lack thereof. The professor was sufficiently protected by First Amendment rights to free speech. Even the university administration, as angry as these leaders might be, had to stand up for the professor's right to free speech. The exchange of ideas, even very abhorrent ideas, is what makes universities great. Would the professor have been fired if he wasn't tenured? That's a question on which we can only speculate. If he wasn't terminated, then perhaps he should have been sued for professional negligence.

In the final analysis, in a situation involving a most repugnant, poorly timed, or ill-advised comment, a tenured professor was essentially protected by constitutional rights to free speech, not by tenure. In even this most radical example, tenure really had limited value.

What are the implications for the thousands of professors who do not make stupid statements at a most inconvenient time? Why do they need tenure? Some would argue that they need protection from capricious administrators above them—department chairs, deans, and provosts—who may take issue with the way they think. Others would argue that in a system based on free expression of ideas and self-governance, it is necessary to protect yourself from those who acquire powerful positions and who use their authority to weed out those who possess conflicting views. In this regard, tenure protects professors from those above them.

Sadly, I have endured such a circumstance where a faculty member in an administrative position went out of his way to make my life miserable. Why would someone waste their time in pejorative action? An answer in this case may reflect the colleague's misguided belief that if I was thoroughly hounded, then I would leave and he would win the favor of the provost. Admittedly the not-so-subtle persecution reached a point that I wondered what my fate would be if I didn't hold tenure.

How many folks outside of academia face this same sort of discrimination from a supervisor at some point in their careers? I believe that a good percentage of all employees—perhaps 30 to 40 percent—may encounter a predatory supervisor at least once in their employment. I've found no research to back up this prediction; it simply is an artifact from talking with non-academics about their careers and their possible intersection with a person they could not please no matter how hard they tried.

An inevitable encounter with a supervisor that is retaliatory for no good reason is all part and parcel of life. Despite my own encounter I remain adamant that it does not rationalize or justify in any way the granting of tenure. I, like so many others outside academia, essentially had to wait it out. Eventually, these bullies and corrupt administrators fail at other aspects of their job, and they are summarily sent packing. But I will also admit it is tough remaining patient when I am the focal point of unwarranted abuse.

In sum, even considering the occasional academic thug who acquires a position of authority within a university, the argument for tenure is quite specious. Essentially, professors want complete protection for speaking their mind regardless of what their criticism might be or whom they might wish to criticize. This argument doesn't align with reality or with the ground rules the rest of society has to abide by to maintain employment. Why should professors be given special consideration in what they do and do not say?

THE INCENTIVE TO BEHAVE BADLY

The vast majority of the working public exercises due diligence in what comes out their mouths; their prudence protects their livelihood. The penalty for capricious and inflammatory statements directed toward customers, co-workers, or those in the chain of command above them is risk of termination. It's this way because there is no guarantee of employment according to the Constitution. No one owes you a job. It is not a right in our society. So long as the legal guidelines of employment are followed, corporations have the ability to act in rather capricious ways, including firing you on the spot.

Think of the disparity here. Each morning a tenured professor gets up and looks forward to a new day. Lingering over a steaming latté, reading the paper, and dwelling on the crossword puzzle, she ruminates about having to go into campus today. Perhaps she will prepare for tomorrow's class, finalize a research questionnaire, or meet with her department chair to complain about the heavy-handed dean. Her day is bright with autonomy. It's merely a matter of her determining what the highest and best use of her day is. She may pause momentarily and ponder on the projected miniscule salary increase the university will purportedly receive from the legislature, but her mind is not the least bit filled with anxiety about whether she will have a job next year.

The professor's counterpart working at Megacorporation awakes very early to finish her chores, drop her child at school, and stop at the cleaners before heading into work. She beats that 8:00 A.M. deadline because she saw what happened to a co-worker in another department who was habitually late. He's still looking for a job in a tight market. She focuses on her tasks at hand, yet there are distracting rumors of a major lay-off happening soon or the plant being totally shut down because its cost structure is several times higher than a sister plant in India. She pauses momentarily wondering where her family will have to move if this happens. Oh well, nothing can be done about it so she refocuses, just thankful that she has her job today.

These two examples offer quite a contrast. A tenured professor lives with much lower risk and greater security. It's a quality of life that most people cannot even begin to imagine. Colleagues will complain about the fact that the tenured professor made the sacrifice and personal investment of years—perhaps a decade or more—to earn the terminal degree and to meet the high requirements of tenure. She's paid her dues; the professor's counterpart never made those sacrifices. That's all true, but what do these arguments have to do with tenure? Tenure was never meant to guarantee a job; it was intended to protect faculty members' professional identity as well as free speech and expression of ideas.

The rest of the world operates with greater risk. Everyday people at work have encounters with those possessing the ability to fire them or the clout to make certain they are terminated for whatever reason—a personal dislike, a predilection to go on a head- trip, envy, fear, you name it. There is no guarantee that a person in a position of authority will not pursue your demise. So long as they don't break the law, there's nothing you can do about it. You don't have tenure.

People respond to incentives. Unfortunately tenure provides the absolutely worst kinds of incentives for professors who already enjoy tremendous autonomy in their jobs. It's time for universities to alter this equation and align academic incentives with the reality that the rest of the world operates under.

Abuses enabled by tenure are legendary and outrageous by any standard of acceptable behavior. Take the case of a professor in a large city with several millions of people and a set of financially challenged universities. The tenured professor was dissatisfied that he wasn't receiving a raise and his standard of living was progressively falling. Using his seniority he badgered his department chair into assigning him to a Monday and Wednesday teaching schedule. Then the professor went across town and signed another academic year contract with a rival university after arranging a Tuesday and Thursday teaching schedule. He simply had to repeat on Tuesday and Thursday what he taught on Mondays and Wednesdays.

Admittedly, abuses of this sort are rare, but it's the more subtle professional changes in faculty that cause alarm. Consider the full professor who simply could not get along with any dean. He was pathologically averse to taking direction, no matter how prudent and gentle, from anyone. Period. This professor arranged for all of his classes to be in the evenings or on weekends so that he could minimize encounters with authority figures such as department chairs and deans. In the private sector this sorry individual would either be remanded to behavioral counseling or (more likely) fired.

Couples who possess tenure may also manifest tendencies to abuse the privilege. The matter is particularly egregious if they are in the same college, or worse yet, the same department. Inevitably the day comes when a committee meeting is called for which they both must attend. If the meeting is primarily informational or if one of the couple has some errands to run, the thought occurs that both of them really don't need to be there. So they agree that one will attend, absorb the meeting's content, and represent them both in expressing their thoughts. All it takes is that one compromise, and the couple has started down a slippery slope from which they will never recover. They begin alternating in attending meetings.

Gradually they observe that they can save lots of time by sharing their presence on campus. Perhaps one will be on campus in the mornings and the other on campus in the afternoons. They make certain that there is enough overlap so that no one will notice. But they far underestimate the powers of observation by their colleagues. Before long there is a standing joke about the hours each keeps. Yet as long as they receive good teaching evaluations and publish periodically, it will be difficult to build a case for revoking their tenure.

As the preceding examples suggest, tenure provides a comfort level that just is not in sync with reality. Someone might argue that the example of the couple with tenure is actually an issue surrounding couples, not an issue of tenure, but I beg to differ. Tenure is the perquisite encouraging the couple to start down the slippery slope toward bad behavior in the first place. Before the university realizes it, the tenured couple has created a new math: $1 + 1 \leq 1$. What business or public agency would tolerate this sort of return on resources invested? What must taxpayers be thinking?

THE DEMISE OF TENURE

How can we save higher education from tenure abuses? The resolution for aligning incentives with reality in academia is so uncomplicated that it's almost embarrassing to even suggest it. *Universities could stop awarding tenure.* That's it in a nutshell—make no further tenure commitments. Stop hiring new faculty on tenure track contracts. If you don't provide the incentive (i.e., tenure), then it can't be abused. As we have seen, it's a pretty fallacious argument that professors need tenure to protect their free speech and full expression of ideas. Tenure is a medieval concept that no longer has currency. It's an innocuous idea that has ruined higher education.

There is no need to take tenure away from those who already possess it, or to remove new faculty from tenure track contracts. Don't bother. *Why incur the legal costs of fighting a battle that is already won?* Let the tenured professorate gradually fade into the sunset as they retire. There's no reason to get worked up over the fact that they have a unique privilege. Let them enjoy their moment in the sun. They will serve as quaint examples of higher education gone badly. Let tenured faculty enjoy what they think is a bodaciously special deal. Tenured professors will soon encounter a new set of highly driven young colleagues—professionals operating under a new set of incentives—whose performance makes theirs look anemic.

As the young, untenured professorate becomes established, they will demonstrate an entirely different mindset, behavior, and productivity. Without tenure, young professors will still enjoy all of the perquisites of a life of the mind, but they predictably won't hide behind tenure and use it as an excuse to underperform. Free of the tenure blanket, young and older faculty will work hard to keep their jobs. They will treat students with respect, they will work diligently to create and disseminate intellectual products, and they will eagerly serve their college, university, and community. Tenured faculty are capable of doing precisely this, it's just that tenure poisons the incentive.

All we have to do is look at the ranks of untenured adjuncts that universities are hiring to appreciate the sort of attitudes and performance we can anticipate by removing tenure. Admittedly universities tend to weigh adjunct faculty down with enormous teaching loads because they are not expected to perform research. But goodness, look at the way adjunct faculty eagerly and effectively go about their jobs. Almost no request is too onerous for them. Plus, they do it at half the cost.

The problem with adjunct teaching faculty is that they normally do not add value to the research mission. They typically make sterling contributions to teaching and service missions. As a result, universities will still need to cultivate a core of faculty who are enduring, who are able to perform teaching, research, and service. How can this be accomplished? How can universities retain the best and the brightest faculty members? If getting rid of tenure means that the core of the enduring faculty is lost, then perhaps getting rid of tenure isn't such a good idea in the first place.

Once again, the best solution is a simple solution. Get rid of tenure, but replace it with extended contracts—say, three to five years in length. I think five years is a perfect compromise because it provides incentive to perform well, and it rewards those that do. If a university has a problem professor, it will be able to cut this debilitating loss in five years at most.

How about professors' fear of retaliation for speaking (or publishing) openly and freely on some topic? Professors already have de facto protection against the abusive department chair, dean, provost, or president. Consider the length of term that most academic administrators tend to serve. Few of the highest-level academic administrators such as presidents, provosts, and deans remain in a position for more than five years. Those that enjoy longevity do so because of their skills and propensity to treat people ethically rather than retaliating against them. Obviously there are occasional exceptions to this generalization, but over the long haul academia says "no" to tyrannical and morally corrupt administrators.

Under an extended contract, such as five years, newly minted Ph.D.s are given a sufficient amount of time to demonstrate that they merit another five-year contract. Although every professor varies in progress toward achieving a promise of distinction in their respective field, most professors who are worthy of receiving tenure demonstrate well before year six (under the current timeline for earning tenure) that they will meet the teaching, research, and service expectations. It's the faculty on the borderline that administrators and their faculty peers have to watch out for. A junior faculty member who does not have a promising performance record at the end of three years is going to have difficulty making the grade at year six. Invariably, marginal cases at tenure continue to produce at marginal levels, and often worse, after receiving tenure.

The beauty of a five-year contract is the incentive for faculty members to continue to be professionally active throughout their careers. For too many faculty members, awarding tenure is a signal that they can somehow slow down and take it easy. That's not the incentive we want to give to intellectually gifted people. Knowing that there is no convenient rationale to cut back, faculty without tenure will simply go about their business of developing intellectual contributions, preparing for and delivering exceptional teaching, and seeking opportunities to serve.

If my proposal to phase out tenure is adopted there will be a transition decade where some faculty members hold tenure and others receive five-year contracts. This induces not-so-subtle peer pressure that could help energize remaining tenured faculty. Those on five-year contracts will be aggressively pursuing teaching, research, and service outcomes. Their commitment and drive should stimulate a reaction on the part of tenured faculty.

If salary raise funds are available, who will receive them? The prospects favor faculty members who are intellectually vital and who demonstrate that they are delivering results consistent with their college's and university's missions. Either the tenured faculty members get with it and produce results, or they stand to earn low raises. Even with 2 to 4 percent raises each year, it doesn't take long for lower-paid junior faculty to achieve equality with low-performing and (formerly) highly paid senior faculty.

How about high-performing faculty members? Aren't they punished by not awarding them tenure? The answer to this question is no. The best and brightest faculty members do not need tenure. To them tenure is a non-issue. Their performance records allow them to enjoy the largesse of the marketplace. They don't need to hide behind the coattails of tenure. They wouldn't dream of altering their research and teaching agendas simply because they have a guaranteed job. These are intellectually vibrant people who do not see their profession as a job or a career; they see their profession as a life.

Won't universities stand to lose their best faculty because they are no longer bound by tenure? Again, the answer is no. Universities do not retain great faculty through tenure. The best and brightest faculty can be awarded tenure at many universities, even at institutions with what may be construed as the highest research, teaching, and service expectations. Too many other factors exist—top leadership, facility and equipment support, quality of colleagues, access to superlative graduate students, endowed position support, staffing—that influence whether a brilliant faculty member will remain with an institution.

How about the mass of faculty who are the core of most universities—those that are capable and who deliver sound performance but who are not leaders in their fields? Without tenure, these valuable faculty members will continue to perform at solid levels, and their employers will make every effort possible to retain them and inspire them to reach better performance. Having never been awarded tenure, these professors will not know what it is like to perform under a dysfunctional form of incentives. The mass of faculty who represent the enduring core of universities will basically perform at higher levels than they would otherwise with tenure.

ALIGN INCENTIVES WITH REALITY

Back in my untenured days I attended a school-wide faculty party on a sunny Sunday afternoon. Several other junior faculty members were standing there with me imbibing a bit of cheap wine while munching tasty treats. It was a beautiful fall day and the semester was well underway. Conversation slowly turned from one thing to another—the fact that our pathetic football team had actually won two games in a row, prospects about the state's economy and salary increases for the coming year, insinuations that the dean would be leaving, and laughter about yet another ludicrous policy coming out of the chancellor's office.

A wisp of wind swirled over us as the conversation turned inevitably, inexorably, toward tenure. One of my colleagues said,

"I just wish they would tell us how many publications we have to have in order to get tenure."

Heads nodded in agreement. Without saying a word or changing my facial expression, I took a sip of rosé and peered over the rim of my plastic cup toward this colleague.

"What's this?" I thought. "What exactly does he mean? He doesn't get it; does he? This isn't about carving notches on a resume. It's about a continuing commitment to the joy of research and teaching. After tenure; then what?"

That moment is emblazoned in my memory. I can still taste the tangy scent of decaying cottonwood leaves in the air and feel the burning warmth of sun on my back as I gradually realized that not everyone saw our profession through the same spectacles. The colleague in question did go on to earn tenure, and he followed that ill-fated decision with the most superlative level of research mediocrity. He did distinguish himself—at being a pain in the ass to any dean that came along. He honed to a fine edge his ability to criticize students, staff, and the professorate and to make fun of female colleagues. He excelled at blocking any meaningful progress by his department in building a better faculty. That's what tenure stimulates—the wrong thinking by the wrong people.

Higher education has such a noble calling and mission to fulfill. Sadly, tenure is an archaic policy that can turn otherwise intelligent people into juvenile sea squirts and in the process consume their brains. It's time to put an end to this predatory behavior and to align faculty incentives with reality.

University faculty members face a wide array of incentives encouraging them to perform at their highest level. They also confront incentives discouraging them from doing the right thing and striving to a higher calling. No incentive has been more insidious in stimulating the wrong behavior than tenure. Remove this perquisite and the academic world will bloom afresh. We will see faculty and administrators pulling together to accomplish what was previously thought to be the unachievable. We will witness the transformation of higher education in a manner that catapults this nation to a new level of esteem around the world—a nation where higher education has enormous respect and that enjoys the support of the public.

Chapter 6

PERFORMANCE ACCOUNTABILITY

Higher education lacks a common language and conceptual framework for the intelligent management of resources. Ideas like production and productivity are as shrill to academics' ears as the term "return on investment." Efficient resource use and added value are concepts that pertain to the filthy world of business, not the hallowed halls of education. Regrettably, higher education is missing the boat by sticking its collective head in the sand regarding concepts and terminology that hold sway throughout the remainder of society. It's a blindness that ultimately will shake the foundations of our ivory towers and create a revolution of momentous proportions.

Academicians may want to run from the inevitable squeeze other sectors have experienced in a global economy, but they can't hide for much longer. Higher education continues to operate as though forces pressuring the rest of society don't have applicability in colleges. Thinking they possess special immunity to these realities that have sharpened the edge of doing business, academics wait patiently, cloistered around each other and ushering lofty platitudes about the severity of change in the real world. They don't soil their hands with issues of money and commerce; they live a life of the mind.

Inexorably economic realities will continue to roll over higher education as it sits passively waiting for the next handout. After all, universities have a lot on their minds—integrating the latest computer technology, diversifying academic programs to serve the needs of a broader set of students, building great athletic teams, conducting esoteric research, and similar big issues. They really don't have the time or inclination to worry about money, or productivity, or efficient resource use. That's small, pedestrian thinking and work reserved for commerce and public management.

If I have slightly overstated the case that higher education just doesn't tend to think in terms of managing resources efficiently, please forgive me. Many academic administrators have witnessed the sudden shift in fiscal premises on which their institutions operate. They have suffered through the erosion of federal and state funding to higher education only to be hit on the side of the head with dramatically lower returns on endowed funds. It's enough to make them want to return to the classroom. These are deeply divisive pressures that are driving wedges among stakeholders in higher education.

BUILDING A COMMON LANGUAGE

Although academic administrators may be highly conversant about the causal forces besieging their institutions and about promising remedies, this doesn't mean that others within their walls are suitably equipped or emotionally ready. It's difficult to discuss nuclear physics if you don't know the language or the concepts. In the same way, any intelligent conversation about increasing resource productivity on college campuses is problematic when a shared language doesn't exist, when concepts of resource management are seen as inimical to higher education itself.

If higher education expects to successfully weather the storm personifying its plight, all stakeholders—faculty, students, staff, trustees, administrators, and alumni—need to be on the same page relative to terminology and concepts. New language and concepts are necessary to facilitate discourse. For example, if the discussion topic is research productivity, then it is essential that we have determined what it means to be productive in each discipline. This will assist a fair discussion of commensurable research productivity.

There is no single best way or easy answer to create a common language within higher education around resource management issues. Perhaps more than anything else, the professorate must embrace the reality of fiscal constraints and move forward in emotionless discussions about the predicament facing their institutions.

At the same time, we need good old-fashioned leadership from academic administrators. They must rapidly bring faculty, staff, and students up to par on terminology, concepts, problems, and feasible solutions. In the end, we are all in this together, or we will be on the outside thinking wistfully about the good old days while former students flock to foreign institutions or private degree mills.

Let's examine an illustration of establishing a common language/conceptual framework and how this language/framework is essential for facilitating discussion and understanding, for helping parties reach the same wavelength.

I made the extremely bad decision of assuming a deanship at the moment that my university went through its first budget crisis. In prior decades we enjoyed progressively larger budgets and above average salary increases (i.e., greater than cost of living increases). We weren't rolling in dough, but there also wasn't a sense of scrimping on every last penny. Ah, the golden haze of those foregone college days. That changed as state revenues dropped like a lead weight with the dot-com fiasco and then doubled downward with outfall from terrorist strikes and the energy crisis.

For all academic units on campus except mine, it was merely a matter of tucking here, cutting there a bit. Everyone was in the same boat, and so psychologically we pulled together in addressing what many assumed would be short-run impacts. Unfortunately, enrollments for my school were increasing dramatically while all others faced declining enrollments. Other colleges could offer fewer course sections by cutting adjunct professors and therefore not harm their core services. But for my unit, this wasn't an option. I either had to add more adjuncts, add more tenured faculty, or cannibalize tenured faculty positions to fund adjuncts. The provost let me know in no uncertain terms that controlling admissions—thereby limiting demand—was not an option. The university needed these student credit hours for future funding.

Thus began a very bizarre dance between us. An important part of the dance was learning how to talk to each other in a civil manner as my unit's problem escalated. We could not afford to cannibalize tenured faculty positions simply to fulfill teaching needs because our accrediting body defined very specific standards regarding full-time faculty coverage and attainment of our research mission. Collaboratively the provost and I tackled this difficult problem. Like other units my college had been assessed an across-the-board 2 percent budget give-back. I couldn't understand why my unit shouldn't be exempt. He couldn't understand why we just didn't leave unfilled faculty positions vacant and use the funds to provide short-run coverage.

We finally began talking on the same wavelength when I started using his office's faculty teaching statistics to underscore my point. Instead of focusing on emotion-filled arguments about perceived needs and aspirations versus inability to reallocate from other units, I created faculty teaching productivity indices for all academic units on campus. The data clearly showed that faculty in my school delivered more student credit hours per tenured faculty member than any other unit. That caught his attention and opened his eyes to the problems we faced.

As a former dean of arts and sciences, he knew that the average tenured faculty member in that college received credit for courses taught by doctoral students and graduate teaching assistants. The tenured faculty in arts and sciences actually spent less time in the classroom than the index of average student credit hours per tenured faculty member implied. He knew this, and I knew this. In contrast, the teaching productivity index for my school was quite solid because our accrediting body stipulated high coverage by full-time tenure track faculty. Almost 75 percent of all student credit hours were delivered by tenured faculty, not adjuncts, graduate assistants, or doctoral students. In short, indices were useful, but they did not quite equate apples and oranges.

Productivity statistics were beneficial in communicating with the provost and in helping others—deans, students, the business community, and faculty—understand the nature of the problem and what might constitute an appropriate resolution. I was very fortunate because this provost understood a performance index when he saw one, even though it might have conceptual and measurement issues, and was willing to concede that the school had a problem. In all honesty, it did nothing to increase the university's funding that he might send our way, and it did not persuade him to reallocate resources except in a very modest way.

Like most provosts who aspire to presidencies, this one soon left, and with his departure came a vacuum of appreciation for the problem my school encountered, the sacrifice we had made to keep enrollments up (thereby raising the university's revenue stream three years down the line), and the continued growth in our enrollments. But most disturbing was the attitude by subsequent provosts that any previously agreed productivity level for my faculty was up for grabs. Successors patently did not quite get it (or wish to understand) concerning the scope and depth of our problem. Communication deteriorated without a common language.

INSTILLING PERFORMANCE ACCOUNTABILITY

A common language and shared concepts about resource management are only the beginning to an end. Rigorous use of measures and benchmarks in assessing performance is enabled by this foundation. Every unit within the academic infrastructure should periodically provide verifiable evidence of progress toward accomplishing goals and objectives. Units should also demonstrate on a routine basis that they are delivering a sufficient return for resources they have been entrusted to manage.

In effect, higher education should move toward more meticulous analysis of operations and outcomes. Universities should be expected to validate that resources are being put to the highest and best use. No homeowner would dream of contracting for a remodel without first reaching an understanding about what work will be done, what standard will prevail, what materials will be used, when results will be achieved, and what the penalties are for poor craftsmanship or delay in meeting the remodel deadline. The same should hold true for higher education, but it doesn't due to the lack of accountability.

In the future, institutions of higher education will be held more accountable for their performance. There are at least two good ways of achieving accountability. Either external agencies such as state legislatures and commissions representing taxpayers can hold universities accountable, or key leaders within universities can mandate the same. As far as any organization is concerned, it is always better to build in accountability than to have an external party tell you what will be done and how you will do it. Consequently, there is good reason to develop a systematic, comprehensive performance review process, a complete organizational audit that is conducted at least once a year.

Many universities lay claim that they have robust audit processes to monitor performance, but what they really mean is that their audit function exists to discover and reveal violations in operating policy. This is an antiquated view of auditing commensurate with a punitive approach to policing people. Contemporary auditing adopts a more constructive view and process. The goal of enlightened auditing is to affirm success in deploying resources, identify areas where resources have not been deployed successfully, and to complete microanalyses where violations in operating policies have occurred.

At the operating unit level—schools, colleges, departments, divisions, staff, and faculty—the goal is to hold people accountable for their use of resources. Those that cannot demonstrate that they are using their resources efficiently and effectively should face the prospects of those resources being reassigned. Talk about a shock to the system! Academic units should lose resources if they cannot demonstrate that they are being effectively deployed to enact important strategies of their university. The resources should be reassigned to some other unit that will provide a higher return, or the unit should receive a sweeping new change in leadership.

For most academics these admonitions smack of business babble. They see such incursions into the sanctity of teaching, research, and service as serious violations of academic freedom. It is precisely this hollow argument that will ensure external retaliation and control. Academic freedom doesn't include the privilege to be wasteful as stewards of the public's trust. If university faculties think such ideas are philosophically opposed to academic freedom, just wait until they see the extent to which onerous external controls are established and how imperfectly they can be applied.

Sensing that it is really to their benefit, academics can begin (at fundamental operating levels) to establish performance measures and systems for maintaining accountability that they can live with, rather than having them imposed. For example, faculty can do the best job of developing measures of teaching, research, and service performance. They may carry on long, egregious arguments in reaching a set of measures, but they know professional standards best, and the constraints of their specific university setting that intimately affects how these standards can be applied. Unless university leaders set in motion comprehensive performance assessment systems, it is unlikely that any single unit will miraculously lead the way. There are too many blatant incentives to keep the status quo.

The implication for all academic units is partaking in periodic performance assessments with the caveat that they first define measures before submitting their operations to periodic reviews. Analysis should help improve decision-making within the respective unit. In the same manner, sub-unit reports should be bundled into unit reports and from there aggregated into even more encompassing reports. The goal is to ensure that all resource investments are reviewed periodically as a basis for decisions about further investments or reallocations to grow other more promising units.

CREATING A PERFORMANCE-ORIENTED MINDSET

If higher education makes more progress in measuring performance and holding people accountable for their performance, many operating efficiencies can occur—sufficient efficiencies to free up millions of dollars in resources that should be better invested in more promising applications. However, mindset plays an important role in explaining why such practices have been eschewed. Consider the following example illustrating how lackadaisical universities become in their stewardship of valuable resources.

My budget officer clicked off her Excel spreadsheet, and we both sat back to chew on our love's labor the last hour and a half. Fall semester class schedules were due next week, and we had just exhausted ourselves looking for any possible slack in the staffing plan. Was any class likely to have enrollments less than twenty students? That was our first target. Our university used a rule of thumb that at least thirteen students in undergraduate sections and at least six students in graduate sections must be enrolled for a course to be offered. Anything less and the class would be dropped. The only sections that came up on our radar screen were three courses that combined undergraduate and graduate students. However, the total enrollments exceeded the minimum of thirteen students.

Next, we turned to our five-year analysis of course enrollments per professor. This spreadsheet helped us to visually track every professor's teaching profile over the previous ten semesters. It was amazing how the same few scoundrels kept trying to scam the system. All you had to do was look at the number of students they taught per class and compare this with the student load of their colleagues. Once these shirkers were identified, then we drilled down to see what courses were planned for them in the coming semester.

It was then just a matter of badgering their department chairs into righting the wrong.

If their colleagues would only review these data they would revolt in less than a heartbeat. Why should they subsidize another professor's cushy teaching schedule? Colleagues unwittingly did so by having to teach more students to make up for their friend's light load. How generous of them to help out in this manner. Yet year after year, the same two professors got away with it. Their department chairs basically didn't want to hassle them, so they spread the pain on the rest of the department.

The worst offender was a horrendous teacher. He was simply awful in the classroom, reading lecture notes based almost solely around the book. Student evaluations were just scathing, especially about his tendency to bully them. He was never available to help students, perpetually too busy trying to scare up a buck out in the business community. In retrospect, he always managed to present a better rationale for keeping the students away from him than assigning him to more classes.

My budget officer and I were satisfied that we had done everything humanly possible to ensure that our college's teaching resources would reach their highest productivity. We had walked through the proposed schedule and compared it to the previous year's semester to ferret out courses that had low enrollment. We had reviewed the tenured faculty's rolling productivity profiles and made a few adjustments accordingly. One fact was certain; enrollments would be up rather than down. This added further to our confidence that a substantial return would accompany the resources invested.

In short, I was more then prepared to attend a meeting the provost had called to discuss teaching coverage. This was one of those meetings you didn't miss if you wanted to retain your job. I felt most comfortable that I could defend our proposed teaching schedule thanks in large measure to my excellent budget officer.

Thursday rolled around, and I found myself walking toward our normal meeting location on a late spring afternoon. Wind-whipped zephyrs caressed me as clouds scudded over head. My thoughts were up in those clouds, thinking forward to the end of the semester and preparing for teaching in the summer. Never any rest.

We gathered solemnly in a conference room—quite a contrast to the sparkling day blowing by outside. Why was everyone so on edge?

I've learned that I never know what to expect when I come to these meetings. I did a quick once-over on my conversation with my budget officer. No reason to hunker down for this one. And then the door opened and in marched the provost, all business this time.

"The university is in a budget crisis, and our job is to do everything possible to make certain that students continue to access classes so that low enrollment today won't result in low funding several years hence under the state's weird funding scheme."

No argument from me there.

The provost then elaborated on the funding facts about which we were all too familiar. He gravitated to course planning for the coming fall semester. Deans fidgeted in their seats. Several avoided eye contact with their boss. It was quite an interesting display of discomfort. I wondered what the hidden agenda was under this subliminal posturing.

"There is one area in which we must make significant progress. I am going to ask my assistant to hand out to each dean their respective underenrolled courses for last fall semester. While she is doing that let me make one point crystal clear. Any dean that fails to make progress in reducing the number of underenrolled courses will face resignation."

This statement set off another spate of shifting and throat-clearing among my colleagues. My school's printout was plopped in front of me.

The provost continued, "You have the data, now do you have any questions?"

I immediately raised a specific point. "The data you supplied for my school is incorrect. It lists three classes as underenrolled. I know for a fact that each of these classes is part of a combined under-graduate/graduate class."

He replied, "Thanks, we will make a note of that."

I wasn't through, however. "Could you please give us a sense of the problem—the magnitude—of underenrolled courses on campus?"

"I'm glad you asked," he said with a frown on his face. "Last fall and spring over 700 classes were underenrolled."

The figure was startling. My academic unit only produced 360 classes every year. We had perhaps one or two classes that at the last moment dropped below the required threshold because of extraneous factors. What were my dean colleagues doing? Seven hundred classes did not meet the minimum enrollment thresholds? This made it very easy on my counterparts' professors who had correspondingly lighter teaching loads. The more that I thought about this, the angrier I became. I was hosing over my faculty by requiring them to vastly exceed the average faculty teaching load without any reward for their sacrifice.

This story illustrates the inherent bias against effective resource management that is often built into universities. No wonder my fellow deans were so uneasy. They had probably known about the magnitude of the problem for years, but they did nothing about it. They had no incentive until the provost indicated that heads would roll. Fortunately this was a big step toward setting things straight. Nonetheless, it also illustrates how relatively unsophisticated university planning and control system are in actuality.

I began to understand that my school's tracking of course enrollment and faculty productivity was something of an aberration. We did it because it was right. Other schools and colleges didn't manage resource intelligently because they didn't have the incentive to. I then began to question what my academic counterparts were doing with their time. If they weren't carefully shepherding resources, what were they doing?

BUILDING RIGOROUS ASSESSMENT MODELS

Annual performance reviews can be a most effective tool for validating performance if conducted and used in a rigorous manner. In universities that advocate periodic and uniformly rigorous reviews, there is great potential to hold people accountable for their performance. The operative word here is "potential." Simply because annual performance reviews are completed doesn't necessarily mean that they will be rigorous, or valuable, in guiding personnel.

An annual performance review is the opportunity to document good performance, to congratulate people for a job well done, and to suggest areas for improvement, just as it can be used to send the opposite message. In this respect, annual performance reviews are valuable for guiding people and their performance.

On the faculty side, and generally less true for staff, is the fact that performance measurement can be ambiguous. Methodologically it is challenging to spell out precisely what constitutes high performance levels by professors when they are responsible for three relatively ambiguous areas—teaching, research, and service. It's difficult enough to define high performance or low performance in any one of these areas, much less reach an assessment for all of them combined.

Commonly agreed-on performance measures do not just happen overnight, they evolve with frustrating discussion that often leads nowhere, leaps of insight that coalesce agreement, progress followed by backsliding as faculty leaders such as chairs receive push-back from their colleagues, and variable application as department chairs rotate within departments. No matter how much research is undertaken regarding what other academic departments are doing (both at a home institution and at peer schools), the models inevitably need tweaking for them to fit and to gain widespread acceptance within a specific university setting.

I've watched assessment criteria for teaching, research, and service evolve continually, receiving a fine-tuning adjust here and a substantial revision there, over a decade and a half. We are still a long way from having the perfect assessment model and measures, but faculty have a very good understanding of what measures are used in each of these performance areas. This helps guide their performance; it creates a common language within the school; and it helps set standards that minimize unproductive grousing about performance ratings. A couple of examples can elucidate these advantages.

The measures we use to assess teaching effectiveness center around written student comments, numerical ratings from student teaching evaluations, course innovations, course grade point averages, number of students served, number of courses taught, number of preparations, instructional development, dissemination of intellectual contributions, and unique achievements (e.g., teaching awards or participation on a teaching journal's editorial board). This is substantial information to massage for every faculty member, but chairs become quite adept at highlighting strengths and shortcomings.

These measures are fairly useful in interdepartmental comparisons when the chair of finance wants to rate one of her faculty members as excellent in teaching because of his courses' rigor. The low grade point average reflects his tough grading and, of course, drives down his student teaching ratings according to this chair. That high teaching rigor is inexorably correlated with adverse student comments and ratings is a patently bogus argument.

The value of having evolved an accepted set of teaching performance measures is the ability to call the finance department chair on her inflated assessment of this faculty member. We merely turn to the marketing department chair and ask about one of his best teachers. This marketing professor routinely reports an average course grade point average of below 2.0 *and* correspondingly superlative teaching ratings. Grading rigor does not necessarily have to come at the expense of student teaching evaluations.

Another example of the evolving nature of performance assessment measures involves service. More attention in our school has focused on defining and improving teaching and research measures than service measures. Quite frankly, most department chairs do not want to hassle their colleagues about service after taking strong positions about teaching and research assessments. Thus, each year the department chairs vow to dig in and get tough about service evaluations, but they always run out of gas after debating assessments on teaching and research.

The end result of this imperfect situation is a willingness by some chairs to laud any intraschool service as above average. Simply by breathing and serving on a committee, whether the faculty member made a meaningful contribution or not, becomes equated with above average service performance. Consider how low this standard is set and the perturbations that follow. Chairs that come in with much more rigorous assessments only roll their eyes and then dramatically raise the service assessments of departmental colleagues to achieve some semblance of equity.

Imprecision in measuring faculty performance becomes a favorite rationale to become lazy. If we can't measure performance accurately, then we shouldn't waste everyone's time in trying. That's a perfect way to never make any progress in the difficult area of performance assessment. A more enlightened attitude suggests that performance assessment evolves, with subsequent iterations successively adding improvements that continue to chase an ideal set of measures and supporting data.

WILLINGNESS TO MAKE TOUGH CALLS

Imprecision also becomes an excuse for not challenging professors about their performance. It's the ambiguous nature of teaching, research, and service that makes annual faculty performance reviews so tenuous. Therefore it is difficult, if not ethically corrupt, to hold faculty members accountable for their performance—or so argue some of the faculty—especially those who don't want to be held accountable for their performance.

Even academic administrators fall into the trap of not wanting to confront faculty about their performance. The hassle is so substantial and the response (or progress) so minimal that department chairs and deans may have a tendency to deemphasize the annual performance review process. Add to this underlying question of ambiguity a prevalent trend of low-to-no raises within higher education, and the problem is greatly compounded. Faculty and chairs rationalize that when there is no potential raise or salary increase available, then why bother to complete the review? All that can result are bad feelings. And we all want to avoid that, don't we?

One of my department chairs once downgraded a professor in an annual review for horrendous teaching. Of the three classes he taught that year (he had a one-semester release for sabbatical), two were rated as mediocre performance and one was rated as horrendous performance. Mind you, we are not just talking about numerical student ratings here. Course materials are reviewed as well as any course innovations. Considered in the reviews is the number of course preparations and courses taught in addition to involvement in curriculum development and leadership for students (e.g., mentoring student professional associations). Chairs examine grade distributions and written student feedback. Class visits are made for untenured faculty. In sum, multidimensional performance assessments are made.

Once the chairs have reviewed the faculty members' annual performance dossiers and made initial evaluation ratings, they meet and go through every faculty member's performance across the entire school. All cases for teaching are considered before moving to research and then to service. The deans and chairs can argue for equity and comparability in these sessions. In this manner, chairs, who make the final performance call, receive diverse input from administrative peers to help them judge what is correct for any given faculty member.

Some weeks after the annual reviews were concluded, this faculty member whose teaching performance was rated low came to me seeking reparation.

"Let me first say that this has nothing to do with money [i.e., the amount of the raise he received]," he began. "I really don't care about the money aspect."

Of course, I read it just the opposite; it *was* about money and the fact that he didn't receive as high a raise as he wanted.

"This is all about my reputation," he continued. "It's about how others look at me."

Since the reviews are confidential unless the faculty member releases the information or unless students really talk down the professor with other students and professors, no one would know.

For the most part, this faculty member's claim that it isn't about money, it's about my reputation was akin to saying that he had taken a vow of poverty when he entered the professorate. His discomfort was all about calling performance like it truly was. He did a less than satisfactory job of teaching for that semester, and his raise reflected this fact. He merely didn't want to be held accountable for his poor performance by receiving a sub-par raise, nor did he want word to leak out that he wasn't a good teacher. Of course, this was nothing new around the school. By now the current student culture (and several student cohorts in the past) had broadly informed other students that this professor was doing (and continued to do) a horrendously poor job of teaching in the classroom.

Yes, he was held accountable for substandard performance, much to his chagrin.

DATA-DRIVEN ASSESSMENT

Tenure and promotion reviews, like annual performance reviews, are another one of the scarce opportunities to hold faculty accountable for results. Battles surrounding these decisions are legendary and hardly need repeating here except to underscore that faculty tend to eschew processes that hold their feet to the fire. Sometimes faculty members appear to be ready to defend colleagues from *any* administrative attempts at applying rigorous standards in cases involving their departments. But these same faculty members tend to be the first to criticize others for their performance.

A fellow dean shared with me her aggravating story about a department of finance that resolutely refused to terminate an untenured professor. Most deans of business schools can easily resonate with tales of woe about her finance faculty. For whatever reason, finance faculty members tend to personify an elitism that is counterproductive to collegial relations. Their journals are the best and journals in other fields are lightweight; their courses are the most rigorous and other courses are pure fluff; their . . . well, you get the picture.

This dean was determined to terminate a junior faculty member in finance who had not completed his dissertation from a well-known East Coast university. He was arrogant and rude to students. He had no publications from his research. No one wanted him to serve on a committee because he acted like a senior faculty member from finance, even at his tender age in the discipline.

This dean prepared diligently for a meeting with the school's' tenure review committee, the committee charged with reviewing contract renewals for untenured faculty members. Certain that the department would once again recommend reappointment, she went armed to present a different case to the committee hoping for the support she would need to convince the provost (who showed no inclination of standing behind tough decisions by deans).

Following proper protocol, the tenure review committee first heard the department chair's arguments for renewing this untenured assistant professor's contract. The chair puffed up to gigantic proportions in exclaiming the virtues of this faculty candidate. He was a graduate of a very distinguished doctoral program on the East Coast; he was completing cutting-edge research that would lead to an international reputation; and his teaching evaluations were beyond reproach. There really wasn't a decision, his performance spoke for itself. Heads nodded around the table, but there was very little discussion.

Next up to bat was the dean. She acknowledged that the assistant professor was attending perhaps the nation's preeminent doctoral program in finance. But the truth be told, he was nowhere near completing his dissertation.

To this accusation the department chair jumped up and slammed his fist on the table saying, "I have personally spoken with his eminent doctoral committee advisor and he is confident the professor will successfully defend his dissertation this coming August."

The dean slowly pulled out a single sheet of paper and distributed copies to the committee members and chair. And then she began: "For those of you who haven't had the time to actually review this file, I have created a list of pronouncements from the department chair, the senior faculty in finance, and the doctoral committee chair at the degree-granting institution. As you can see, over four years ago when the finance department presented the case for hiring this faculty member, the doctoral committee chair predicted that the candidate would defend his dissertation within the year. In fact he did not."

"*Every year for the last three years*, the department chair and senior faculty have submitted their written opinions that the candidate should be granted a contract extension because he would successfully defend his dissertation by year's end. Each year, the doctoral committee chair indicated that the dissertation would also be successfully defended. As you know from carefully reading his file [which, by the way, had not been checked out by any of the tenure review committee members from the dean's assistant for any of the past three years], all of these pronouncements are carefully documented. I have accurately summarized them."

And so, she ended, "As you can see, there is no further basis to renew this contract."

The committee agreed entirely with the dean and pronounced that it would not recommend contract renewal. The chair of the finance department left seething.

I asked her if she was afraid of the political repercussions from undermining the department chair. With great wisdom, she replied, "Sometimes faculty refuse to see the facts even when they are staring them in the face. Finance faculty members tend to blow smoke about their discipline's rigor and the accomplishments they achieve. But in the end, they are no different than other faculty. I had nothing to lose by telling the truth except to win affirmation from the tenure review committee. As to the finance department chair, I have nothing to win or lose there—I'm not from finance and thus will never be his peer."

Everyone is for accountability in performance so long as it is the other person whose record is soundly criticized. Faculty members, like everyone else, tend to think that they are performing well and don't need to undergo annual reviews. They cite the demeaning nature of annual performance reviews and how they are inconsistent with building collegiality. They harangue about the incommensurability of teaching, research, and service and how performances among faculty members should not be compared due to inherent imprecision of assessment tools and measures. They will go so far as to rearrange facts to fit with their perceptual framework. These and many other defensive techniques make accountability difficult. But they do not represent sufficient reason to forego performance assessments. In actuality, they are precisely the reason why such assessments are desperately needed in the higher education context.

The rest of the world suffers through annual job evaluations. Few people have the luxury of not being evaluated. Many perform a craft, trade, or profession in which it is difficult to measure with great precision the entire scope of performance over a year period. Their complex jobs defy easy assessment. It is often problematic to distill results into an intelligible summary that can be communicated with others. In some cases, outcomes from their performance may not be available for years. Nonetheless, performance assessments are still made despite these ambiguities.

Academicians would like others to think that the work they do is so unusual, so intellectually challenging, and so diverse in terms of outcomes produced that performance assessment doesn't apply to them. To this, we can say hogwash. If you can assess the performance of a physician or a parent who cares for children, then you can also assess academicians.

ACCOUNTABILITY AS A FRAMEWORK FOR IMPROVEMENT

Higher education will continue to drift along on its tremendous resource base constantly begging for more unless we insist on receiving superior performance. Taxpayers, legislators, and government leaders are primed to demand more, much more, from public institutions of higher education. In private institutions add to this mix strong pressure from trustees and alumni who have a vested interest in seeing their institutions deliver a higher return on resources invested.

By holding higher education to a higher standard of accountability, the details will rapidly take care of themselves. It is much less difficult to determine what separates good performance from substandard performance if finely honed assessment systems are in place and methodically functioning. Universities that do not create systematic, comprehensive performance reviews cannot make a strong case for holding people accountable. And unless assessments occur with regular frequency, it will be difficult to craft a system of incentives to improve performance. Faculty, staff, and academic administrators will recognize opportunities to circumvent the process and will capitalize on them accordingly.

Performance assessment and accountability go hand in hand when striving to achieve continuous improvement in institutions of higher learning. These initiatives provide the basis for making more intelligent decisions at all levels, decisions that lead to higher and better use of valuable resources. As with many worthwhile endeavors, the beginning of this sojourn requires hard work and caution in navigating the sea of emotional turmoil and mass of inertia resisting change at any cost. Nonetheless, the disarray associated with the early phases will pay off in the long run, and it's to this destination that we must hold our rudder firm, free from distraction.

Faculty, in particular, must be cognizant of the costs of maintaining their comfortable status quo. Although they may be content with the tranquil way things are in their department and college, they fail to see that performance assessment and accountability should lead to a vastly improved context in which to teach and complete research. Instead, they often disdain change because of potential disruptions to a context in which everything is oh-so-comfortable.

Some small but important aspect of performance, such as holding office hours, serves as an excellent case in point regarding how assessment can lead to dramatic negative implications for faculty perquisites.

Faculty members typically are very accessible to students. In fact, these days with electronic networking, some faculty members argue that students may have too much access. Inundated with emails, a faculty member can literally spend all day communicating and not devote sufficient time to course preparation, research, or service. It is interesting to observe that a quick phone call or text message would often save valuable time over documentation required in an e-mail. Greater precision is normally needed in e-mails compared to phone calls given the lasting electronic record created over the Internet.

Some professors have accepted that e-mailing can serve as a viable surrogate for office hours. Accordingly these professors are a little more lax in setting up a wide range of office hours, especially if they work at home and use the Internet to provide near-simultaneous interactions with students. Here is where trouble begins to brew.

A university where I was a faculty member ran into problems with professors not being available for office hours. Central administration did not enforce a systematic, comprehensive adherence to posted office hours. It simply managed by a squeaky wheel policy. When a professor violated office hours, students would complain to the department chair, and the chair would remediate the problem. There was no concerted effort to assess this dimension of faculty performance, and university leaders felt the number of complaints were quite small.

Enter *The Princeton Review*.

The Princeton Review, an independent education services company best known for test preparation materials, is a completely free-standing guide that rates colleges and universities on various dimensions of performance. No college pays a fee to be included in the survey. *The Princeton Review* rates colleges on a wide variety of dimensions that are informative to prospective students such as food, professor accessibility, social activities, athletics, environmental practices, and academics, to name a few. *The Princeton Review* surveys 120,000 students primarily using electronic methods (95 percent) and paper surveys (5 percent). An eighty-question survey probes into issues surrounding a college's campus life, academics, and administration, among other factors noted above.

The Best 368 Colleges is a special publication published since 1992 on top colleges. One issue it endeavors to inform prospective students about is professor accessibility. This became the rub for my employer because of all 368 colleges assessed in that year, my university was ranked number one for having the least accessible professors of all top colleges.

Think carefully about this dubious distinction for a minute.

All a professor has to do is comply with her or his posted office hours for students to leave with an impression that faculty are accessible. That's it. Show up for work when you say you will show up for work. This is by no means rocket science. Millions of employed people have to follow this simple rule during their work week. Showing up is 99 percent of the effort required to leave a great impression.

Performance assessment had led to a new wrinkle at my university and an outcry from the community. Why aren't faculty members in their offices? What responsibility do they have to taxpayers to hold office hours given the salary they receive? Is this a widespread phenomenon across campus, or is there a rogue pool of offenders in a college or colleges? These and many other questions immediately surfaced. Moreover the president and regents were facing a public relations nightmare.

The faculty senate president tried to put a positive spin on the situation by cleverly deflecting attention to the university's strong ratings for academics and student opportunities in the review. The local newspaper wasn't about to buy that specious argument, noting, "But when you are singled out with the top ranking in 'professors make themselves scarce,' and you throw in rankings for 'professors get low marks' (eighteenth last year, fourteenth this year), it's time to go back to school."

Faculty had become too comfortable with their jobs and lifestyles. Independent assessment and monitoring corrected poor performance. Pressure is intense for faculty to hold liberal office hours and for professors to be in their offices during these published times. Most important, accountability became a clear mandate for improvement.

In the preceding case, assessment and accountability enabled improved use of existing resources. In other instances performance assessment can unearth resources for reinvestment in programs that enhance student learning, faculty professional development, and community service. Performance assessment can be a two-edged sword. For example, professors might be surprised to discover that past resistance to performance assessment and accountability has prevented progress in the very areas that they hold to be so sacrosanct.

By assuming responsibility for ensuring accountability, faculty members provide leadership commensurate with the highest aspirations of their profession and the academy of scholars. It's time for professors to meld together in a collective push to enhance how resources at their institutions of higher learning are made productive. To be certain, staff, academic administrators, and trustees are significant collaborators in this process. Nonetheless, it is to the faculty that we must turn for the insights and motivation to raise higher education to an altogether higher level of respect and contribution to bettering the human condition.

Chapter 7

CULTIVATING A STRATEGY SUPPORTIVE CULTURE

W e once lived in the North Valley of Albuquerque, a bucolic section of the city along the muddy Rio Grande river. Small ranches, outlandishly tasteful as well as tasteless trophy homes, modest suburban enclaves, and hovels nestle cheek by ruddy jowl along shady lanes of luminescent cottonwoods and elms. Acequias, or earthen water canals, radiate from the mother river spreading life to verdant green alfalfa fields, red and golden delicious apple trees, and ubiquitous chilé crops. Horses and horse flies abound, lending a distinct farmland character to surrounding bohemian neighborhoods.

Fowl are plentiful whether boisterous roosters calling in predawn hours, raucous blue jays darting through the canopy, hummingbirds trolling for trumpet vines, gawky sandhill cranes and rotund Canadian geese commandeering fields during winter, or ever-present crows and ravens ruling the treetops. They're attracted by the Rio Grande's bosque, a mixture of cottonwood trees and native vegetation, such as four-wing salt bush, chamisa, and Apache plume. Birds also shelter in tamarisk and Russian olive trees that are striving to dominate the indigenous ecosystem.

Virtually every morning when leaving home, we ran smack into an enormous flock of guinea fowl on a nearby street. My wife hums a short trumpeting prelude and ceremoniously announces, "There's the faculty."

Our day is a little richer, a little lighter, for seeing guinea fowl on the loose, for their inability to be intimidated by cars as they saunter across the street, and for their awful ungainly ugliness—faces only guinea hens could love.

They've chosen to roost together in a towering ponderosa pine tree in front of a house whose yard is littered with their copious droppings. Our community flock of guinea fowl spends each night high in the tree defecating on those lower in the pecking order, a similarity to faculty that does not go unnoticed. They perch throughout the pine's branches feeling a measure of safety in a ruthless world, aloof in their ponderosa tower.

Descending in the morning, they first soak up sunny warmth on the black asphalt street, preening and fluffing to overcome night's chill. Then they migrate across the road to a neighboring house with its expansive lawn. There the guinea fowl hunt and peck for little tidbits and morsels before heading out for serious foraging. An orange tabby crouches smack dab in the middle of the lawn hoping for an opportunity to catch one off guard, but the guineas pay it little mind. They have it surrounded thirty-to-one and the cat knows from hideous experience what happens if it tries to get nasty.

All appears to be well and good in the life of the North Valley's guinea fowl. There's apparently a lot of food to eat because their population continues to grow slowly and flocks divide. The most threatening predators are stealthy coyotes, brazen cats, aggressive dogs, and unconscionable cars, but these hazards are safely managed by the large number of observant eyes. Truly horrendous weather seldom descends on the tranquil habitat. There's sufficient water in the acequias. Life's good.

But there's just one little rub, and here is where the parable of the guinea fowl has remarkable congruence with university faculty. For whatever reason, guinea fowl cannot leave each other alone. If one is pecking in the grass for a tasty morsel, then two others will immediately rush over to steal its treat, leaving that poor individual battered and bruised.

If another guinea fowl has the misfortune of innocently glancing in another's direction, this glance will detonate an explosive retaliation completely out of proportion with the offense. It will be attacked belligerently by the offended counterpart. Punishment usually consists of being chased for several yards before falling victim to a bout of vicious pecking.

In short, guinea fowl just can't get along. They're never satisfied. They want what the others have. They bully and intimidate to get their way. They fight and connive until they win a pyrrhic victory. And on obtaining whatever it is that they want, guinea fowl are grossly dissatisfied.

THE CULTURE OF UNIVERSITY FACULTY

Yes, faculty members are a lot like guinea fowl, or at least they behave like guinea fowl. If someone understands this little fact, then they are miles ahead in knowing how to work effectively with faculty members. I say "work with" because you can never "manage" faculty given the archaic system of collective governance and tenure perquisites dominating universities today. Administrators can only hope to work with them, not manage them.

I once reported to a top academic officer who absolutely, positively hated the faculty. The normal term he used for his colleagues was the "f**king faculty." He would anguish about behaviors that he saw as idiotic, lament about their silly antics in the classroom, ponder the faculty senate's inability to make progress on anything except a faculty club, talk disparagingly about their greed, accentuate their personal corruption, laugh condescendingly about their scholarly insignificance, and generally not have much nice to say about them. Oh, to be certain, there were exceptional scholars—and deeply good women and men—that in his sight merited admiration and glowing words, but that was a pretty limited set.

The peculiarities of faculty are legendary, quite innocent, colorful, and, although aggravating, easily overlooked. Thus, it came as more than a mild shock when my boss—the chief academic officer, the top academic representative—soundly trashed faculty under his aegis. Did he forget his roots? He began his plodding climb up the academic ladder as an assistant professor. He put his time in as a faculty member and has been graced by opportunities to provide leadership. That's quite an honor—to serve as the academic leader for hundreds, sometimes thousands, of intellectually gifted individuals.

However, there is a much more significant point to be made relative to anyone's condescending attitude toward the professorate. No department chair, dean, provost, president, regent, department, school, or university can get anything accomplished without the cooperation of the faculty. Students may be one of a university's most significantly vital customers (among taxpayers, the business community, and other key constituents), but the faculty is the most important internal customer. They teach the classes, impart the knowledge, conduct the research, and accomplish the goals of any university. They add substantial worth to students while guiding them to aspire to lifelong education.

Without a doubt, university faculty members are a very unusual lot, that is quite clear. They are horrendously independent. Academics tend to think in long, convoluted circles. No question to them is really an easy question. They will see all sorts of angles and fine nuances that trip them up from ushering forth a simplistic answer. So they are always qualifying their responses.

Inherently distrusting anyone in an administrative position, they hold back as a bit of paranoia sweeps over them even when you exchange greetings. A cheery "Good morning, Professor" will leave that faculty member wondering, "Now, what did she mean by that? What's so good about it? Does she know something I don't know? The skies are actually quite cloudy. What's good about that? Does she know that my manuscript was just rejected by that top tier journal? Is she rubbing it in?"

And as you turn down the hall, you've left behind a great mind churning wildly to ferret out hidden insinuations from a well-meaning administrator.

Professors' most endearing characteristic is the tendency to be lost in space. All that brain power is continually massaging a teaching or research problem. They may be physically present and even carrying on a conversation with you, but their minds are elsewhere. Their great love of intellectualizing may appear to make them rude and discourteous, but they really mean no harm. They're just focused on solving huge important problems in their minds, or at least what they see as big problems associated with their esoteric research.

This tendency to be focusing elsewhere, heads in the clouds and where abouts unknown, can come back to haunt them in momentous ways that they usually don't grasp. In my capacity of fund- and friend-raising, I happened on a very wealthy individual whose family member had just been rescued by our medical system from tertiary-level cancer. He was profoundly humbled and willing to do whatever he could do to eradicate this insidious disease.

His center of attention on battling cancer came up during a luncheon at which I thought I would be pitching our university's eminent arts program. As he related the gruesome details of his wife's diagnosis and long road through treatment and recovery, I listened very carefully. At the same time, I was rapidly rewriting what I would tell him about star programs emerging at our university. However, by the time he had completed his story, a look of weary exhaustion commandeered his face. Deep in his heart, he wanted to do everything possible to prevent others from going down this road of battling cancer.

At moments like this when someone exposes their innermost thoughts and emotional scars I believe it is ethically essential to move beyond my intended reason for a luncheon (i.e., cultivation of a donor for a possible gift) and above all be sensitive to the integrity of my friend.

When he cut into his entrée, he asked, "Well . . . what's happing over at our favorite university?"

I admitted to him that we were making incredible progress in a variety of areas, particularly cancer research. And I added that I would like to share about a very special research project and clinical researcher, but at a different time and place. Now was not the moment to belabor him with details of our aspirations. We agreed to meet the following Wednesday at 7:00 A.M. to discuss the matter further.

Driving back to my office I thought quickly about the potential. This gentleman could easily afford an endowed chair in the $3 to $5 million range. We had an eminent cancer researcher that we wanted to retain on our faculty. He loved our university. All of these signs spoke to a convenient intersection of enabling factors. All I needed to do now was to assemble the documentation for a presentation.

I quickly dialed our star professor. His voice mail kicked in, so I left a message about the luck of finding a wealthy donor who might support him and his research. All I needed was an updated resume. I then repeated all of this with a more detailed email.

A day went by with no response.

The following day I phoned him and conveniently connected. I let him know that this gift opportunity was almost a sure shot. He could end up with an endowed chair and support for his research for years to come.

He promised to get his resume right out to me. I indicated that this would be great because my next meeting with the donor was now only six days away.

The day before the meeting I still didn't have the resume, so I called the professor to no avail. I emailed an emphatic note. And then I moved to Plan B about the arts center.

The next morning I presented Plan B to the donor.

The point of this little scenario is to underscore how detached faculty members can become due to their intense focus on their research and teaching. Some may think this is a quaint, some would say cute, characteristic of academia. But in this case, it cost a valued researcher (and my university) an endowed chair.

Perhaps I and others shouldn't be offended by these faculty eccentricities, and I shouldn't take it personally. Professors generally do not mean to insult others by their detachment. However, if I acted this way when they or anyone from the community want something, they would bristle. I've found that a double standard often exits. If they are late for an appointment, I need to understand that they were busy solving global warming while they drove to work. If they entirely miss an appointment I shouldn't take it too hard, they got caught up in analyzing data that finally began to fall into place. Hey, mellow out, it isn't that big of a deal. Of course, if I am late for an appointment or skip a meeting with them, they will be all over me. Well . . . I guess that's just the way the world works. But it doesn't have to if we strive for a positive culture supporting every person.

The Value of a Strategy Supportive Culture

A daunting challenge for higher education is to harness faculty talent in accomplishing the goals of specific academic units and the goals of the university while vastly enriching our society. A simple solution for the problems confronting higher education is to instill a strategy supportive culture; that is, a common set of values, beliefs, mores, philosophies, and generally accepted ways of behaving that enables universities to fulfill their missions and to achieve their strategic objectives.

A number of tactics are crucial in this quest for a strategy supportive culture. University faculties are not like bison or cattle; they are people. You work with people, you manage cattle. To achieve a strategy supportive culture you must work with faculty. You must win them to your side—help them see the benefit of pursuing and achieving goals, a mission, and a vision that are mutually defined. You don't order them around (although you can try this short-sighted approach without much long-run success); you work with them to gain their confidence, respect, and cooperation. You set high standards and then adhere to those standards while having compassion for those that fall short.

In short, building a strategy supportive culture is a very arduous, ambiguous, and taxing task facing academic administrators. It is a task that high-level administrators often never quite comprehend, or if they get the message, they do not know how to achieve or they fail to make progress due to other pressing matters. Yet once a strategy supportive culture is in place, the sky is the limit in terms of what results can be achieved. Just look at high-performing universities. These are the benchmarks where distinctive cultures have been inculcated. But culture is elusive; it can come crashing down if not properly nourished. Following are some approaches for building and maintaining distinctive strategy supportive cultures in higher education.

HONOR THE PAST, BUILD FOR THE FUTURE

Universities resemble large aircraft carriers. They are cumbersome to navigate, and academic administrators must anticipate directional changes miles in advance. Merely turning the rudder will not result in any appreciable change of direction. You're fighting the inertia of a huge mass with incredible momentum already progressing on a specific vector. At cruising speed, a pilot is not going to turn that puppy on a dime, to say the least.

Consequently, when a change in direction is desired the captain makes an assessment of where the aircraft carrier has been and where it is currently headed. After taking these readings, extensive preparations are initiated, such as: Crew members are alerted about the change in course to come, orders are given to change engine speed, environmental conditions are assessed (e.g., wind, water depth, wave patterns, and height of swells), and a reading is taken on surrounding vessels (i.e., Is the coast clear?). Only after prudently reading these factors (and others) can orders be given to initiate change.

The analogy of an aircraft carrier is extraordinarily apropos to universities and leadership efforts to guide them. They cannot be turned on a dime; they have enormous momentum that cannot be quickly dissipated. Leaders (i.e., pilots and captains) can only achieve navigational changes by working with others. Many internal and external contextual factors constrain possible changes in direction, and competition may already be filling the desired space or target position.

Those responsible for building strategy supportive cultures in universities are wise to remember this analogy. In particular, university leaders should realize that change cannot be achieved without the cooperation of those who form the institution. Unlike aircraft carriers, universities are primarily comprised of people—faculty, students, and staff rather than massive amounts of steel and machines—who have a significant stake in where *their* institution is headed. They possess an appreciation of where the university has been and where it may be going. They may resist a change of direction unless leaders involve them effectively in that change.

Back in my days as an assistant professor, one of my dear friends from our doctoral program began the third year of his first faculty position. Catching up over the phone, he said that he was a bit distraught because no sooner had he completed his initial year, the dean resigned. In his second year, a search was completed for a replacement. A new dean was hired, and everyone looked forward to a bright new period in the school's history—an infusion of fresh thinking about the long term.

The departing dean had done all of the heavy lifting by negotiating an additional half-million dollars in new faculty positions. The only immediate crisis facing the school was a looming accreditation visit. My friend recounted the vast amount of introspection, negotiation, and consensus building that occurred over the prior two years as senior faculty reviewed and revised the school's strategic plan. The accrediting body stipulated that all schools must be mission-driven. They would be required to demonstrate that they had adopted an appropriate mission, and they must produce evidence that decisions are mission-based. As a junior faculty member, my colleague had been spared from much of the political infighting and extensive work surrounding the school's effort to meet reaccreditation.

My friend gushed over the prospects of hiring additional new faculty in his discipline. According to the school's strategic and hiring plans, his department would receive two new tenure track positions. This allocation reaffirmed his decision three years before to join the faculty. His department was beginning to achieve a prominent name nationally, and the addition of two colleagues would strengthen participation in academic societies, expand the diversity of research, and provide drastically needed coverage in concentration courses. Merely recruiting for new faculty would send a powerful message that his program was on an upward trajectory.

His new dean landed with a miserable thud. After only three weeks on the job, the new dean informed the department chairs that the school's mission needed to be improved. He felt that it needed more focus, so he would be disseminating a new mission statement that he wanted the faculty to adopt. Faculty members were aghast. Very careful attention had gone into the progressive refinement of the mission and strategic plan since the previous reaccreditation effort five years earlier. Input for changes was solicited from a broad array of internal and external constituents—students, the community, alumni, advisory boards, and central administration, among others. A midpoint review was undertaken by an external review team of seasoned deans who were closely affiliated with the accrediting body.

The faculty began to whisper about the intelligence of the new dean—a tendency to be intellectually challenged—and the wisdom of changing things at this late stage in the ballgame. Some began to question his experience and leadership. But the story didn't stop there.

My friend snorted with acidic laughter as he replayed the new dean's next folly. It seems that the one department always causing the most turmoil in the school—the one that went out of its way to block progress toward reaccreditation—had covertly captured the new dean's ear. The senior faculty in this department cajoled the dean into reassigning new faculty positions to grow an initiative they had in mind. My friend's department was losing two new faculty positions. He said this was an exceedingly bitter pill to swallow; his senior faculty colleagues went to the provost.

I commiserated with his loss, but he stopped me dead in my tracks. The lunacy didn't end there. The new dean indicated to the chairs that he was going to change how endowed faculty lectureships and professorships were assigned. He didn't like the several-decades-old policies and forthwith would determine who received them as well as how much of the spendable earnings they would be awarded. Although many deans with the cooperation of the faculty had refined the policies and processes for awarding endowed positions over the years, the new dean wanted control—including leaving donors out of the information solicitation loop when considering endowments.

Chuckling out loud, I asked whether his new dean had a death wish.

"No," replied my friend, "But there is already talk of a vote of no confidence. Imagine only weeks out of the starting gate and we're ready to trash him."

"The probability of that happening is pretty small isn't it?," I interjected.

"Wrong," said my friend. "The new dean has decided to reallocate half of future summer research funds for faculty to seed funding for academic program development. We are more than united to tell this bozo to chuck it. His honeymoon is over."

After I hung up the phone, I could only shake my head. This was a textbook case of how not to do it, how not to introduce change at a critical time. My friend's school had one major bogey in the center of its radar screen—achieving reaccreditation. This incoming missile deserved completely undivided attention. The faculty needed to pull together for the impending accreditation visit. The last thing you want to convey to an external review team is the impression of infighting and disagreement over the mission statement and strategic plan.

At a time when the new dean desperately needed to provide leadership and to bring faculty members together, he managed to accomplish the exact opposite. He fractionated the faculty. Instead of using a high-powered rifle to aim squarely for the target's center, he employed a shotgun to blast away at what he thought the problems were before sufficiently soliciting input and feedback. He managed to turn a slam dunk into a major loss.

The moral of this story is quite plain. It's desired, even prudent, to inject change. Heaven knows that higher education needs it. But change should be part of an enlightened process toward building a strategy supportive culture. You don't honor the past and build for the future by coming in and implementing a scorched earth policy. That's how you create a non-supportive culture.

Things tend to be the way they are in organizations for specific reasons. Therefore, it is equally as important to understand the rationale underlying the status quo as it is to formulate a correct reading on the future direction that should be taken. You don't get from point A to point B without taking lots of intermediary steps. This is certainly the case for academia.

Leaders need to be decisive, but they also should balance action with a judicious reading of past history and present conditions. It will be very difficult to lead toward a strategy supportive culture if you have stepped on everybody along the way. As the captain of an aircraft carrier understands, you must encourage people to work with you because if that doesn't happen, disastrous results will occur. Take the time to achieve a judicious reading. Contemplate feedback and input solicited from many constituents and stake-holders. After preparing everyone for change and having won their goodwill, only then will efforts at building a strategy supportive culture have the best probability of succeeding.

REAP WHAT YOU REWARD

Although academics are loath to admit it, they respond to incentives. The hoary myth of academia would have the public believe that faculty members live only for their students, for their love of research, for passionate discourse, and for pursuit of truth. In fact, academics are attracted to higher education for all of these reasons *and more.* They enjoy incredible flexibility in their hours each week. Many agree to work on the basis of nine-month contracts and so have summers free for their hearts' desire. They enjoy self-governance.

Of course, all of the great aspects of academia are balanced by some negative conditions. Salary and pay rates are very low. Aspiring faculty devote years to receiving the proper credentials and then must serve a lengthy apprenticeship before they enter the secure senior ranks. They seldom leave their job at the office because their profession challenges them to think constantly about research and teaching issues. Perquisites are limited at many institutions. There are seldom sufficient resources to support professional development. Budget and salary increases tend to be modest to nil. In short, it's not all red wine and roses being a faculty member.

In building a strategy supportive culture, academic leaders must be very cautious about the incentives and disincentives used to influence behavior in their universities.

Remember that we tend to reap what we reward, even though we may not intentionally be communicating a reward. The following example illustrates how quickly things can get out of hand when faculty members sense a golden opportunity.

A regional private university hired a new provost. After one year on the job, she looked at her span of control and realized she wasn't getting as much done as she wanted to because she had too many people reporting to her. Included among the many deans was a division of health policy. This faculty group was not sanctioned as a full-fledged college or school due to a long historical battle. A prior president had cleverly started the program against the advice of various deans and the faculty senate. Several decades later emotions still were raw.

The provost summarily assigned the division of health policy to the dean of arts and sciences. Rather than integrating the division within the existing department of political science, she declared that the division would continue to remain an autonomous academic unit. Not everyone was happy, especially the dean of arts and sciences, but the division settled into place. The dean recognized that the division had a reputation for incredible infighting and backbiting. Some considered the unit almost unmanageable, but he would do his best.

Six months later the provost left for an opportunity at a more prestigious university. Enter another new provost. While this provost was busy getting his footing, faculty in the division of health policy cleverly went to the faculty senate and passed a resolution mandating that the division be reconstituted as a separate college (reporting to the dean of arts and sciences). Health policy faculty members in the new college were overjoyed. They had their own school and their own director who reported to a dean rather than the provost. They pretty much controlled their own destiny without the scrutiny of the provost.

Because faculty members often act like guinea fowl, the inevitable backbiting began to resurface. A university audit raised allegations of budget mismanagement by the director. A new director was summarily assigned by the dean of arts and sciences—an associate dean—because the school of health policy had no viable faculty candidate. Buoyed by the audit, the associate dean instituted control to achieve consistency between the school of health policy and all other departments in the college of arts and sciences.

Order reigned. Faculty in the school of health policy groused a bit, but improvements in the academic unit continued to evolve.

One faculty member within the school of health policy just could not tolerate the associate dean who was serving as director. She complained to her colleagues. She complained to the school's advisory board members. She complained to department chairs and faculty within the college of arts and sciences. She complained to the dean. Not one single person agreed with her complaints. They were totally ungrounded; everyone else realized that she wanted to take control, to become director.

The faculty member in question tried to schedule an appointment with the deputy provost to complain to him. He declined, indicating that he stood firmly behind the dean and associate dean of arts and sciences. He was willing to meet, but only if the dean and associate dean attended the proposed meeting. She was irate and then covertly made an appointment with the provost. Rather than first checking with the associate dean/director, the dean, or the deputy provost, the provost met with her and sympathized with her complaints. The door was open and she repeatedly visited the provost making wild accusations and demanding change.

Finally the provost grew tired of hearing her complaints and unilaterally decided to move the school of health policy to another school—the college of business. The provost did not first seek input from the dean of the college of business, or any of his colleagues—deputy provost, dean, and associate dean (of arts and sciences). Faculty members in the school of health policy were in turmoil causing a great ruckus. Their anger was matched by the dean of the college of business, who simply refused to take responsibility for the school of health policy.

Things simmered for a while. The school of health policy was constantly embattled. One more time the faculty member worked her magic by convincing the provost to remove the associate dean and reinstitute the former director of the school of health policy (under whom the adverse audit occurred). The provost was never informed about this audit deficiency because it occurred before he assumed his post. But he also failed to make the effort to understand the long, convoluted history of the school of health policy.

Now the fox was back guarding the hen house.

This heartrending tale illustrates that we reap what we reward. The deputy provost brilliantly understood the concept of incentives. If he allowed a faculty member with a reputation for unjustifiable complaining to meet with him alone, he would send a clear message that he didn't stand behind the associate dean/director and dean. He would send a message that it's acceptable for faculty to do an end run anytime they have a complaint. In very short order, he would be managing the school of health policy rather than the associate dean/director or the dean of arts and sciences.

This tale has very serious repercussions for establishing a positive culture in that private university. At least as far as academic leadership is concerned, the provost jeopardized the very integrity of functional working relationships. This is not the type of culture that enables an entire team to take on tough issues in the future. Bad behavior on the part of a single faculty member has been rewarded, and now the team reaps the downside of this bad behavior as it becomes less cohesive, lacking trust.

A strategy supportive culture operates under a fundamental set of assumptions about behavior. Implicit is an overarching context of incentives and disincentives that motivate people—faculty, staff, students, alumni, community stakeholders, and central administrative leaders—to attain institutional goals. Academic administrators have to be very careful in the decisions they make and the policies they follow to send the proper messages.

In the final analysis, people are people. They may be a most brilliant student, an internationally recognized scholar, or a coveted teacher. Beneath these facades, they are just ordinary individuals trying to make their way through an ambiguous and uncertain world. Never underestimate their penchant for aligning (their) behavior with the incentives they encounter. Fortunately, academic administrators can use these propensities to their advantage. They can also align incentives with the sort of strategy they seek to execute and create cultures that build high performance in institutions of higher learning.

BUILD CONSENSUS, BUT PLEASE, MAKE DECISIONS

Ray Stata served as chairman of the board and former CEO of Analog Devices in Massachusetts. His firm enjoyed a huge measure of success and when explaining some of the causal factors for this fortuitous occurrence Stata pointed to a blend of decisiveness and consensus-based planning (Stata, 1988). Analog Devices merged bottom-up participative planning with top-down directives. In Stata's view, a strategic plan is stronger when it originates from a single source of inspiration, but it is enabled when many have input because they ultimately execute the plan.

The academic environment presents many obstacles to achieving a blend of consensus-based operations and planning with more authoritarian overtones. Given collegial governance, where faculties have direct input into the selection of department chairs and deans, such a blend is often quite difficult to instill. At any point faculty members of a college or academic department can issue a vote of no confidence, thus depreciating authority and hindering management by academic administrators of those units.

The consensus dictum is so ingrained within academic cultures that administrators tend to hide behind the safety of faculty governance. They use consensus-based processes to delay making decisions, especially concerning thorny issues that may create dissension. Operating under the premise that consensus is paramount to their retention of faculty goodwill, some administrators will avoid tackling any divisive matter simply to perpetuate their administration. This administrative cowardice may fool many sheep, but the more insightful will press provosts, deans, and department chairs to lead, follow, or get out of the way.

I was once a faculty member in a department comprised of twelve colleagues. Due to the continuing evolution of the professional discipline, our degree program required periodic review and revision. The latest challenge centered on our student internship requirement. Our department chair led a number of faculty meetings regarding recent trends in the industry and reactions by other leading degree programs. The top programs seemed to be gravitating toward a six-month internship as opposed to a one-year internship that we required.

The department chair clearly felt compelled to lead our degree program to the top of the field. Although discussions continually circled back to the wisdom of sticking with the one-year internship, the chair reminded us about the impact such rigidity could have. A one-year requirement would undoubtedly chase some very promising students to our competitors. One-year assignments were becoming increasingly difficult to locate given budget reductions in the industry. A dated curriculum could have a deleterious impact on academic rankings.

After continued heated discussions and flip-flopping by colleagues regarding the best approach to take, the department chair admonished us that we had ducked the issue too long. We were wasting time and needed to either alter our degree requirement by adopting a six-month internship or stick with the one-year expectation. Yet as academics, we sensed that consensus was lacking. We were entirely uncomfortable with moving forward.

It was a dreary rainy day as we filed into our large conference room and laid the internship issue to rest. Gone was the light banter of respectful colleagues who enjoyed each other's company both professionally and socially. Eye contact was at a minimum. Most hid behind enormous coffee cups or buried their heads in a newspaper, feigning interest in what was going on outside the ivy-covered walls. Ten minutes later the choice was put to faculty vote and paper ballots submitted. Results were tallied: seven votes in favor of the six-month internship and five votes in favor of the one-year internship. The decision was made. The department chair had his way.

For the next two weeks, the halls were surprisingly quite about the decision. Although the vote didn't split us apart, it also did nothing to pull us together. As might be expected, a couple of colleagues, the most vocal and critical of the change, groused about the demise of our great program. But, in time, even they went silent as we returned to the business of the semester.

The announcement of another department meeting two weeks later came as quite a surprise because we had been meeting almost continually. What this time? The agenda was not distributed in advance. We were simply told to show up.

On the appointed day, we gathered once again in the confining bleak conference room. Once a vibrant off-white, years had added a dingy gray patina to the room's walls. Decades-old furniture—battered, broken, and bruised—surrounded a dented oval table. We took our favorite seats with questioning eyes and curious minds. One of the most senior professors inquired if anyone knew what this was about. His question was met by silence and heads wagging "no."

Our department chair strolled in with his jaw set. There was no prelude, no humorous antidote. Normally he singled out someone who had just reached a major achievement, but not this morning.

The chair got right into it. He said that he appreciated all of the discussion regarding the change in our internship. He thanked the majority who voted to support the six-month internship as the correct direction for our program. However, despite the positive vote, he felt that too many of us had voted simply to support him, rather than voting for what they believed to be correct.

In an impressive display of decisiveness, the chair indicated he would accept the faculty vote only as a recommendation. He thanked us for submitting our opinions via the vote, but he decided to overrule this recommendation. Our one-year internship would stand. On that he adjourned the meeting.

Over the course of the following weeks, an amazing transformation occurred in the department. A dismal malaise that hung over our interactions lifted. Colleagues were sharing in the fullness of their appreciation for each other. But even more startling was the renewed respect the faculty held for the department chair. Surprisingly, his longtime critics mellowed their complaints. His decisive action had returned us to consensus, although it meant that he had to go against what he thought best for our degree. It takes a big person to make this kind of decision.

In the end there was virtually no adverse impact from sticking with the one-year internship. In fact, other leading programs began to reverse their strategy as well. They had been caught up in the superficial drive to emulate what other programs were doing rather than thinking about what is best for graduates. And our department chair? He continued to enjoy our respect, admiration, and support in negotiating the balance of his appointment.

GUIDE RATHER THAN MICROMANAGE

A strategy supportive culture is noted for its ability to involve people comprehensively in executing tactics pertinent to the strategic plan. It's all about making certain that everyone is on board, in agreement with the strategic plan, and willing to commit to its attainment. Clearly this is a very challenging goal for academic administrators due to decentralized governance and participative decision-making. These environments call for careful direction setting and a willingness to recognize that the best strategy execution occurs at the lowest level.

Universities need insightful leaders who are able to articulate a compelling vision for their organization and to build consensus about the underlying mission, strategic objectives, and strategies for achieving the overarching plan. But execution of the plan must be delegated. Given the scale of operations for most universities, top echelon leaders should not expect to become overly involved with strategy execution except in providing general guidance. Instead top leaders such as regents, presidents, and provosts possess the responsibility for ensuring that strategic goals are achieved. They oversee the control function while letting those at operating levels—deans, department chairs, faculty, and staff—determine how strategies are implemented to attain the objectives.

Since universities rely on participative decision-making, leadership style should match this culture. This implies more of an oversight function by academic administrators rather than strict operational involvement. Leaders should provide guidance and do everything possible to eschew micromanaging. Direct control over operational decisions runs contrary to a culture of consensual decision-making and collegial governance. Micromanaging does little to reinforce a philosophy of decentralization that's so important in academic environments. It hinders innovation at operating levels.

A dean of an engineering school at a private university once confronted the prospects of rapidly growing enrollments. Students were attracted to great job opportunities this school provided and the deep slate of corporate recruiters. Firms were seeking graduates who wanted high-paying positions in desirable locations of the country. Success in enrollments does not always imply organizational success, and in this instance, higher enrollment created a severe problem. His university was unable to fund new faculty positions due to fiscal shortcomings across campus.

As this dean related his story to me, he spent many sleepless nights trying to figure out the right combination to this thorny puzzle. If he asked faculty to teach more courses, then they stood to lose the excellent faculty that had taken so many years to build. If he pestered the president for additional faculty positions, he could well end up back on the faculty providing part of the solution. If he increased admissions standards, thereby lowering the number of student admissions, he would incense students, parents, and alumni. He was at wits' end until he just let go.

The dean was driving himself crazy trying to solve a problem that really wasn't his. Department chairs are responsible for staffing courses and offering sufficient course sections to meet student demand. Rather than trying to figure out what his school would do in accommodating the many students, the dean quit micromanaging. He turned the matter over to the department chairs while providing an incentive to resolve the enrollment dilemma. This was a pretty clever approach.

At his next meeting with his three department chairs, the dean reviewed the basic dilemma confronting the school (i.e., too many students) and the constraints (i.e., no additional budget and internal and external stakeholder expectations that students are able to access the courses they need). Next he discussed the numerous goals of the school—teaching, research, and service and how they were simultaneously compatible and contradictory given resource support by the university.

The dean calculated a specific target number of students that each faculty member must teach for the school to provide coverage given course demand. To this point faculty had been teaching four courses each year, two per semester. They had been clamoring for fewer courses so that their research would improve. As a result, the dean defined a single guideline and left it up to the chairs to determine how they would reach the goal.

According to his calculations, the average faculty member should teach at least 120 students per year to cover demand. The dean told his department chairs that as long as faculty in every department taught an average of 120 students, then it was permissible for faculty to have a three course per year teaching load. In short, the dean provided a guideline and then did not micromanage. He turned the matter over to the chairs to solve. They just sat there, stunned, and then agreed to come back the next week after discussing it with their faculty members—same time, same place—and explain how they would address the problem.

The following week, the chair of the electrical and computer engineering department pitched a fit. "I need three more faculty lines as it currently stands just to meet demand. I can't lower teaching loads and meet the projected demand. I simply need more faculty positions." The dean expected to hear such an inane reaction from this particular department. These faculty members were notorious for blocking progress and thinking entirely within a tiny box.

Next the chair of the mechanical engineering department shared her discussion with faculty. "My colleagues are quite eager to reach the three course teaching load. We have three vacant faculty positions that we have been recruiting for and we would like to terminate those searches. Instead, we will hire six full-time lecturers to provide coverage and wait to see whether the president will be able to provide additional funding next year. Ideally we will phase out two full-time lecturers for each of the following three years and replace them with tenure-track faculty, and we will seek two new full-time lecturers to cover the additional demand. This way everyone wins—students, faculty, and university."

The dean thanked her for her innovative approach and threw a questioning glance at the chair of electrical and computer engineering. Next was the chair from civil engineering. "My faculty members have decided to assign just two professors to cover each of the introductory core classes. They will each teach six sections of class next year with substantial assistance from graduate teaching assistants. Neither faculty member will be expected to complete any research. These covenants will be reflected in their annual performance evaluations. Next year, two more faculty members will take on this teaching assignment, and the following year two more faculty members will follow. We expect that our faculty will only have a concentrated teaching year once every twelve years."

As this case illustrates, the dean set a guideline and then refrained from micromanaging. The problem of execution was left to the faculty and department chairs. They are smart people, they will figure out how to achieve a difficult goal if they are provided some incentive. This approach is consistent with decentralized decision-making. Move the operating problem to the lowest level to ensure that the culture is strategy supportive. There are so many creative ways of solving the difficult problems that micromanaging isn't required. Provide guidance; micromanage as a last resort.

The dean can anticipate some resistance from the department of electrical and computer engineering. He simply needs to provide oversight and intervene if the department fails to deliver the target of teaching 120 students per faculty member on average.

What better approach to take than aligning incentives with strategic goals? Ordering chairs and faculty members to teach specific classes with specific enrollments only turns the dean into a department chair and violates the notion of building a strategy supportive culture. Department chairs are hired to resolve problems by working with their colleagues. Let the faculty decide how they will execute a strategy to accomplish a goal—that's how you build a strategy supportive culture.

COLLEGIAL GOVERNANCE REQUIRES COLLEGIAL ADMINISTRATION

I was sitting at a nicely decorated table in the university's sumptuous faculty club waiting for a colleague to join me for lunch. The appointments were very tasteful, and the atmosphere reeked of genteel charm. It made me wonder why the university was able to afford such lavish confines for the faculty club but could pay me so little in terms of salary. I concluded that this perquisite must be part of my salary. Simultaneously, as my thoughts began to run a little darker, in walked my friend with another colleague in tow.

I was introduced to a faculty member from another college, the largest college in terms of faculty and students enrolled on campus. It's always nice to meet someone from outside your school and a convenient way to compare faculty environments. Such exchanges help you understand the equitability of teaching loads, access to research opportunities, and peculiarities of administrative régimes. Our conversational prelude to lunch was quite pleasant as we exchanged little tidbits about our backgrounds, research obsessions, and professional aspirations. But once lunch arrived, things changed in a hurry.

Dean longevity at her college averaged something on the order of two years during the last decade. Recently the faculty had selected an internal candidate who showed vast potential and who knew where all the skeletons were hidden. Finally, here was a person who could work within the strange governance system of the college and cater to the demands of central administration without selling the college short. The college would now make important headway with alumni and the community in fundraising.

According to my new acquaintance, that was the forecast six months ago. The honeymoon was already over despite blazingly phenomenal success in raising endowed lectureships and professorships. The dean showed an amazing proclivity for convincing wealthy alumni, local businesses, and people of means in the community that they desperately needed to shower money on the college. Already five endowed lectureships and three endowed professorships had been added to the college's meager portfolio of distinguished academic positions. These perpetual funds would help provide a smidgen of additional salary support for faculty who were underpaid compared to the college's competitive peers.

To the same extent that the dean could do absolutely no wrong in fundraising, he also demonstrated an uncanny sensitivity to the faculty's governance idiosyncrasies. The faculty governed this college, plain and simple. Decisions and polices were formulated and approved by the faculty, period. Deans implemented faculty policy, they didn't make policy. The college prided itself on consensus-based operations. Faculty members would far prefer investing five hours at a faculty meeting to ensure that everyone had a say and that conflicts were resolved than leave angry after a short one-hour meeting.

The dean was willing to work within this structure. He had a strong enough ego and a penchant for insightful leadership that meshed perfectly with a setting that drove other deans—insensitive transplants—crazy. Rather than fight the faculty about who had most authority, the dean simply worked with them while going about his business. After all, he was focused on results, not fleeting questions of who possessed the most authority or who controlled whom.

"Please pass the salad dressing," I requested of my new acquaintance. Sadly, the luxurious confines of the faculty club could not mask the fact that our food was prepared in the same kitchen serving the student union. More salad dressing was required to rehydrate my dried-out grilled chicken commandeering the bed of wilted lettuce and greens. I lavished the chicken with a smothering load of dressing, doubling the fat calories originally planned for this meal.

Squelching a burp and almost gagging on the Sahara Desert–dry chicken, I just couldn't contain myself any longer.

"Let me see if I have a correct reading on what you have been saying. Your new dean has brought in more endowed funding than any of his predecessors—he's more than doubled the college's endowment in his first year. He also honors the consensus-based traditions of faculty governance, acting more as a mentor and guide rather than tyrannical leader." The colleague nodded vigorously in complete agreement.

"So, what's the problem?"

The new dean had made two very critical mistakes. He selected not one, but three associate deans. The college had always traditionally managed with one. Worse yet, he selected three aggressively condescending males who were already running roughshod over the faculty. They didn't respect, much less tolerate, consensus-based decision-making. Rather than honoring the time-honored culture of faculty governance, they blatantly bullied things through, much to the faculty's dismay.

To compound the matter, they were progressively driving a wedge between the dean and the faculty—they constituted the wedge. Given their immediate access to the dean's ear, they convinced him to buy brand new furniture for the administrative suites and then cajoled him into moving to another building distantly removed from the majority of faculty offices. It was a matter of record that buying new furniture was the kiss of death. It symbolized greed and self-centeredness that faculty despise. The previous dean, who expended precious college funds on new furniture for the office, was summarily sent packing within the year.

One of the associate deans possessed a brilliant mind and silver tongue. He thought and spoke with lightning speed when on his feet. Faculty members were intimidated by his intellectual prowess and condescending attitude. In faculty meetings, he verbally whipped opponents, humiliating them in the process. Underlying this extraordinary capacity was more than a hint of sadistic evil; demons lurked beneath his smooth superficial facade that occasionally escaped—an ugliness that repulsed his colleagues.

"Excuse me," I interrupted my new colleague, "but don't the other associate deans help to balance this excess?"

"Oh no," she snickered. "One has an equally pejorative nature. His modus operandi is browbeating people into submission. Female faculty members sense just a hint of abuse—physical intimidation— every time they have an exchange with him. Furthermore, he will do almost anything, say almost anything, for money. There's nothing my faculty colleagues hate more than overt glorification of the almighty dollar. He would sell the college in an instant if he thought it would benefit his pocketbook. And he would lie about it all the way to the bank."

"The third associate dean is renowned for saying what the dean wants to hear and then stabbing the dean in the back. Despite being treated to a wonderful salary increase, this associate dean is sullen. There is only one thing on his mind—taking over as dean."

By the time she had finished with her tales of woe, we were nearing the end of our meal. I had to run to class, so I couldn't remain to hear more about the crisis facing her college. But I didn't need, or want, to hear more. Her sharing helped to convince me that I didn't really have it that bad. Sure, our dean was sort of a buffoon, but he was a kind one. Perhaps I shouldn't be so hard on him for failing to differentiate more among the faculty when it came to salary raise monies and research support. Yes, just maybe I had better keep my critical thoughts to myself from now on.

Fast forward six months. Fall semester was only one month from completion. Semester break loomed on the horizon—the golden time when I could refocus on my research. I picked up the campus newspaper on my way into the office one morning expecting to read a litany of excuses about why the football team had done so poorly this year. For paying our coaches so much, they sure fail to produce results equivalent with their salaries. Instead the headline touted the football team's progress this year and projected a winning season next year. Go figure.

On the bottom right corner of the front page (illustrating what really matters as far as students are concerned) emblazoned in black bold type was a sub-headline reading, "College Dean Returns to Faculty." Scrambling to my desk I laid out the paper and read about the sudden resignation of the dean I came to know over a dry salad some six months earlier. The article was very brief. In January the dean would be returning to the classroom along with his administrative team. Details were lacking, but it appeared that the dean had given central administration an offer it couldn't refuse, an offer no doubt orchestrated by the evil empire—his compatriots—the associate deans.

A strategy supportive culture requires consistency between faculty governance and faculty administration. The type of administrative style adopted by academic leaders is largely contingent on an academic unit's culture, governance, and approach to decision- and policy-making. With the predominance of collegially based cultures within higher education, it is appropriate to adopt administrative styles mimicking this cultural predisposition.

The preceding vignette illustrates just how tenuous administrative currency is within universities. Excelling in one and even two areas, such as fundraising and sensitivity to faculty beliefs, is insufficient if an administrator or administrative team fails to honor cultural traditions. For further confirmation we only need to look to a prominent business school in the Rocky Mountains where a new dean raised a startling sum of $35 million during his initial two years. However, he was summarily trashed by his faculty because he didn't spend enough time with them; he was too busy out there raising money.

Strategy supportive cultures inevitably seek to walk the razor's edge between what faculty want and what their administrative leaders want. Compromises must be made by both sides if they intend to live up to their full potential. Some might question whether these compromises don't undermine the ability of an academic unit to reach its full potential. However, another more cogent argument suggests that cultures and administrations evolve over time. By balancing strategy, culture, and administrative style, probabilities increase that high performance will ensue. Outcomes are increasingly the focal point for higher education. High performance and academic cultures able to produce such results are ultimately the solution the public expects from both private and public academic institutions.

Chapter 8

TOUGH LOVE FOR CUSTOMERS

Higher education serves a complex mix of internal and external customers. Not surprisingly, it is extremely difficult to satisfy external customers without first attending to the internal customers. When universities satisfy their three primary internal customers—students, alumni, and faculty—they are more likely to meet the expectations of key external customers such as organizations that hire graduates, taxpayers who provide federal and state teaching/research funding, and society that consumes intellectual and cultural property created within the ivy-covered walls.

Universities fundamentally consist of (present and past) students and faculty sharing various educational products, services, processes, and outcomes. Buildings, land, equipment, and infrastructure support, in contrast, are assets that facilitate education. Without students and faculty there is no university. Remaining is a collection of physical and infrastructure resources looking for some mission to support.

Unlike most other organizations, the end products of universities—alumni—represent a continuing valuable relationship. Alumni are a valuable asset regardless of whether direct communication occurs. Alumni represent the direct sum total—the value added—of each university's educational effort. A university's educational value is also distributed to society in the form of intellectual contributions from teaching and research. These contributions are disseminated in diverse ways ranging from academic journals to conferences to theatrical or artistic performances.

Because of their unique customer relationship with past students, universities progressively contribute to society through alumni despite less than efficacious contact with alumni. This is how many leading universities achieve greatness. At any point in time they are performing inspiring teaching and research that adds value to current students (and to society), and their past products—alumni—are contributing to society through their knowledge, skills, expertise, critical thinking, insights, ethics, and other personal assets culti- vated (in part) at their alma mater.

Many universities find themselves in their present state of fiscal disarray because they have been too generous with their internal customers, too giving and lenient. Higher education has not set high enough expectations for internal customers. In many respects this has been caused by society's drive to provide a college educa- tion to everyone at low-to-no cost. As any parent knows, when off- spring receive things/rewards/perquisites without working for them, they tend to appreciate them (both the good or service and the parents) a lot less. It's time for balanced reciprocity.

Higher education vitally needs an infusion of tough love for inter- nal customers to overcome its descending spiral toward mediocrity and slow deterioration. Tough love—setting high expectations and achieving high value in return—can balance the equation and build a collaborative drive toward excellence. And who—university, alumni, students, or faculty—is against excellence? Every university should aspire to a superior reputation of meeting external and internal cus- tomers' highest expectations. The same holds true for university expec- tations of alumni, students, and faculty.

ALUMNI

I once ingratiated myself beyond the realm of all possibility by informing the chancellor of a leading private university that his alumni giving rate of 30 percent wasn't good enough. He looked like I had slapped him in the face when informed that his alumni were shirking their responsibility to build an even greater institu- tion. Needless to say he was livid, absolutely livid. Back came all manner of defensive statements about how this was an extraordi- nary rate for most academic institutions, and how his alumni prided themselves on their generosity. He argued that his institution was beating peers in the rate of alumni giving and the increasing rate of their giving. After all, what was happening at my institution that gave me room to criticize?

He had a point, but not a good one. First, I wasn't criticizing his institution's results or even its fundraising efforts. I was merely trying to point out that as long as we see a 30 percent participation rate as "good," then we will make very slow progress toward achieving 100 percent. Second, he tried to defend his "good" rate by comparing it to the miserable rate at my institution. This was an unfortunate comparison of an apple to an orange. His was a private university, mine was a public institution. The advantage was clearly on his side.

The chancellor was so caught up in defending his alumni's supposedly great rate of giving that he only paused for a second when I mentioned that a target of 100 percent was achievable through tough love. Clearly he was intrigued by both the goal of total participation and what I meant by tough love. Nonetheless, like so many academic administrators he had to defend the realm. So he missed a golden opportunity to think out of his box, if even for only a second, in a manner that might have led to sweeping changes in alumni relations. He passed by the opportunities to instill dramatic improvements in giving and to establish his institution as *the* preeminent university among peers—the best of the best.

Universities need to do a much better job of informing their students *before they graduate* about commitments enlightened alumni are expected to fulfill. Among many possible contributions and options, alumni can:

- Identify and channel high-quality prospective students to their university and to a specific college
- Work with employers in their communities to identify internships and co-op opportunities for students of their alma mater
- Volunteer to serve as an alumni leader for their geographical area
- Encourage leading professionals to speak to classes at their alma mater
- Communicate a testimonial about the value of the college's degree
- Volunteer to mentor a student
- Volunteer to speak to a class
- Identify employment opportunities (jobs) in their community for graduates of their alma mater
- Assist graduates in their professional relocation to their community by volunteering as a professional contact

- Provide financial support for students or faculty through the following:

  1. Institute an annual contribution for general operations
  2. Make a specific donation for capital equipment
  3. Establish an endowed fund for student and faculty scholarships
  4. Donate a specific amount for a one-time scholarship
  5. Include their college in their will
  6. Establish a donation that challenges friends and family to match this contribution

Note it isn't *just* about giving money; it's about alumni investing in an institution and alumni investing in themselves.

We shouldn't automatically anticipate that alumni will magically rise to the occasion and annually send a large donation. That's because no one has ever taught them what it means to be an alumnus or how they might return something to the institution that increased their value, broadly defined. Nonetheless, many universities wait until students graduate before they begin to cultivate a meaningful relationship. That's far too late, as many astute private institutions of higher education will testify. The real pros already have students making pledges before they graduate.

It's critical to accentuate the importance of viewing alumni reciprocity as more than just giving money, although donating money is a nice way to express gratitude. Alumni have so many valuable resources and means for helping their alma mater. But these doors won't be opened (as wide) if alumni sense that all a university wants from them is cash or a big gift on their death. People want to support institutions that play an important, fundamental role in their personal development. They want to aspire to do higher things for their universities, but not when they are treated simply as a checkbook or open wallet.

In this regard universities can also do a better job of explaining the advantages they receive as alumni including:

- Staying connected with a vibrant intellectual community
- Capitalizing on a large network of alumni
- Accessing promising talent for their organization
- Retaining personal and professional relationships with alumni in their cohort

- Participating in the continuing improvement of curriculum and student services
- Sharing knowledge and wisdom with aspiring graduates
- Accessing expert seminars in their field
- Participating in fun alumni events
- Helping their alma mater improve the value of its degrees
- Providing guidance to impressionable minds
- Enabling others to access intellectual opportunities they otherwise cannot afford
- Enjoying the satisfaction of building a better college

In short, alumni have many ways to benefit from maintaining close relations with their institution of higher learning.

Building alumni relations begins before students are even admitted. Showing respectful interest before students enter the doors or land on campus is a harbinger of great alumni relations. There are so many opportunities to build this relationship after the initial letter of acceptance is sent to the lucky candidate that they defy description. Yet before you know it, the requisite length of study has been completed and these students are walking across the stage at convocation.

No, setting expectations for alumni doesn't happen after students graduate; it happens before. And it's more, so much more, than just having the dean, president, or alumni president say a good word of cheer and intimating that they will receive letters after graduating asking for assistance to make the university a recognized stand-out. Those initiatives are essential, but they are only part of a much bigger picture of relationship building that ultimately determines how generous alumni will be with their time, talent, and resources.

More than any other predictor, the quality of students' experiences explains how freely they will give immediately after graduating, decades after graduating, and when they pass on. The overall quality of their college experience has enormous influence on alumni perceptions of value added, of the worth of their degree, and of the justification for investing those years in earning it. This is a daunting realization. It isn't just one factor that universities can focus on in building superb alumni relations. They have to address all of the facets in receiving an education.

This overall "quality of experience" is extremely difficult for many universities to cultivate these days with students working so many hours while earning their degrees. Attending college is just one of several things that the vast majority of students try to balance in the course of their lives. Family, job, and personal interests outside of education may have higher priority than working toward a degree. Consequently, these competing priorities tend to dilute and even tarnish the university experience. Campus becomes just another place that students benignly check into during their week. The length of time it takes to receive their degree exacerbates the banality of university experiences.

So it will take more than a great football team, superlative job offers, bodacious parties, cutting-edge academics, engaging student body, awesome weather, or awe-inspiring dorms to leave an indelible sense of place and experience with alumni. It all has to be just right for alumni to think that they experienced the best years of their lives, perhaps the best years they will ever experience in the course of their lives.

In the course of deaning, I have had the privilege of meeting alumni who just cannot thank the university enough for how deeply their lives were touched. These alums typically graduated forty and fifty years ago, when the university itself was quite small and the school's enrollment proportionately modest. Their eyes sparkle when they retell the tales of those days—tales that when heard are really quite commonplace. Each story merely represents one bright moment, but each coalesces to form an integral part of a larger chain of events that left them almost breathless and transformed as women and men.

The distinguishing factors were not the physical facilities of the university at that time, after all the buildings were quite modest by standards even in those days. It wasn't necessarily the fine weather embracing the campus because some of their favorite tales involve winter blizzards of heroic proportions. The athletic program was still evolving, and the university was fortunate to even field a team back in World War II and the postwar era. Some recount fond friendships from sororities and fraternities, but the Greek system has never amounted to much on our campus. Some alums dwell on a favorite professor or class in which they learned a very big lesson for their lives.

No, there isn't one particular factor that these cohorts of alumni point to as the causal reason underlying an extraordinary experience. Rather it is the entire ensemble of factors where they felt like a very significant member of a small community—faculty, deans, and student colleagues sharing in the great mystery and joy of becoming more enlightened, not only through academic content and thought processes but also about the way of life.

Tough love for alumni implies setting expectations about the nature of their relationship to the university and their responsibility to reciprocate. Many universities, especially private institutions, use alumni to organize and lead campaigns at maintaining relations. There is no intervention quite like alumni soliciting peers on behalf of their institution. Such networks are very effective in communications and maintaining contact.

Without educating future graduates about what it means to fulfill alumni expectations, colleges and universities cast their fate to the wind. They hope to connect with alumni in the future and in the process cling to the dream that alumni will toss a few resources their way. That's a pretty presumptuous and disorganized way of conducting business. It's also one that has a very low probability of paying off. Graduates begin to disconnect before they even receive their diploma. Without an effective infrastructure for continuing alumni development, why do universities think that their graduates will shower them with gifts when there are so many great causes pleading for money these days?

To illustrate the behavior universities do not want to encourage, I am reminded of the development example I heard about from another dean. He was lamenting the fact that only 19 percent of alumni at his university send in some form of donation. This had a very real impact on his operations. Of the funds submitted, the majority was targeted toward student scholarships rather than general operations. He concluded that it is easy to raise student scholarships, but it is very difficult to raise discretionary funding.

He was particularly nonplussed by a recent graduate he befriended. She had received over $12,500 per year in student scholarship support from his college alone, and a substantial amount from the university as a whole. Costs of attending his college per year, exclusive of living expenses, averaged about $6,000. While a student she had held a job with an accounting firm, earning a decent annual salary on the order of $40,000. After receiving her degree she took a plum job at the same firm for $70,000 per year.

This student was lavished with financial support from her alma mater. Her studies added value to her abilities and eventually this led to a great job. This case has all of the characteristics of a great alumna/university relationship in the making. So I asked the dean what giving pattern she had established in return for the generosity so kindly bestowed by his college. He swallowed hard, a grim sneer came over his face, and then he informed me that her giving last year was $25.

Think of it? She could only manage to write a check of $25 to show her gratitude? Somewhere along the line this dean, or a predecessor, had worked to raise $250,000 from some source—corporate or alumni—to form an endowment that would spin off $12,500 in earnings a year (at a 5 percent spending distribution) to support this ingrate. She was an accountant, presumably someone who understands the value of money and the fact that it doesn't grow on trees. She should be embarrassed.

Bleeding hearts out there may postulate that she is a single mother with two children and thus cannot afford to give back fiscally right now. She will pay back these funds in the future; please be patient. But I had to chuckle after thinking precisely these thoughts. My friend indicated that one day he inadvertently stopped for a breather and was looking out on the fine day unfolding just beyond his plate glass windows. Up into the college's parking lot drove this student—still six months away from graduating—in a hot-off-the-lot luxurious upscale Japanese brand car. Perhaps she just borrowed it for the day from her parents, I suggested? No, it had a university permit affixed on the windshield.

This dean obviously needs to institute a program of tough love for his students to prepare them to function as productive alumni. So many students ride for virtually free throughout their education—they don't appreciate this great gift. A college degree has become an entitlement rather than a privilege, and consequently graduates do not perceive that they have any responsibility to demonstrate appreciation beyond token giving for the generosity they have received.

I was about to turn away from my discussion with this dean when he lightly caught my arm and said his story wasn't over. Two days after watching this princess drive into the college's parking lot in her new wheels, the university hosted an alumni reception.

He was chatting with a few middle-aged alums who had driven across several states to attend homecoming. It was delightful conversation about their good times and subsequent success they felt they had been blessed with after graduating. He made a mental note to check their giving history the next morning.

Suddenly a small young lady came from behind and introduced herself as a graduate. She wanted to share her appreciation for the degree she had earned and how it had opened doors leading to the fine job she had just landed in city administration. The dean told me he was taken back by the tears in her eyes. She and five brothers had immigrated to the United States from Mexico. The brothers had gone into construction despite her encouragement to them to attend college. She was a single mother who clawed her way through the degree program, never earning high academic honors. Yet on graduation she began a life of prosperity that her brothers and family had never known.

This is a graduate who will make certain her children earn their college degrees. She will make her contribution back to my friend's college if he only makes the effort to remain in contact with her and to periodically solicit support. She didn't possess an entitlement mentality; she realized how fortunate she was to earn a degree that would pay off repeatedly after graduation. We agreed that this graduate would give far more of her meager resources than the one who received the generous ride but who didn't have a clue about her responsibility to give back.

Alumni are as valuable a resource to universities as universities are to alumni. A fulfilling relationship fostering reciprocity can benefit both alums and a university. But experience suggests universities must constantly seek ways to nurture these relationships. As alumni remain engaged and participate in initiatives that grow a better institution, numerous opportunities arise to inform them about the inherent value of building strength in their alma mater.

Tough love for alumni implies first building a healthy relationship with consistent communication and involvement in university activities. After this base is established, every effort must be made to educate alumni about the continuing benefits a strong relationship means for them personally, as well as for their institutions. With assistance from alumni leaders, a wide range of expectations can be outlined that help graduates reinvest appropriately in one of the most important institutions affecting their lives.

STUDENTS

Students who are successful in their studies ultimately become alumni. The best way to build a strong relationship with alumni is to deliver a spectacular educational experience to them as students. With this realization in mind, universities are stretching themselves in many creative ways to deliver first-rate customer service. The breadth and depth of the tactics being used in the name of customer service are mind-boggling. Many center around students' living environments on campus, where amenities take the rough edge off dormitory life and mimic off-campus apartments and rental housing.

Other strategies focus on creating a comfortable base for the mass of students who commute. The idea is to facilitate their access to campus (especially convenient parking) and to nurture an inviting atmosphere once ensconced in their studies and between-class activities. Designing student union buildings that offer first-rate meal service, enclaves for socializing, entertainment, and study portals is an illustrative tactic universities are putting into play to enhance customer relations. But the initiatives are much more comprehensive than just fancy student union buildings. Physical recreation opportunities are being upgraded as well as academic student services in the drive to solidify exemplary relations.

Attitudes on campus have gradually shifted from viewing students as a captive audience to appreciating them as customers. This change has been long overdue—students have historically been treated like, well, like students. Similar to businesses, universities now attempt to put the customer first. This is an admirable and lofty ambition and justly deserved. The only problem is that universities tend to forget that they are also the customer of students—there is an inviolable reciprocity.

Universities have swung the customer service pendulum so far to one extreme that they have lost sight of the academic responsibilities they must uphold. The concept of "the customer is always right" should pertain to nonacademic campus services and efficient processing of academic student services, *but not necessarily to academic curricula, pedagogy, and standards.* Unfortunately this is often not the case and skillful students wise in a world that is competing for their dollars know exactly how to push the right buttons on the academic side.

Universities particularly need to demonstrate tough love in matters concerning admissions (and retention) and the classroom. They should not confuse maintaining high academic standards with disinterest in customer service. In fact, high academic standards can be equated with high customer service because without high educational standards a university's degrees have little inherent value. Thus, when a university does not admit a graduate student with powerful community ties but substandard test scores, customer service is enhanced to all of those students who did meet the criteria. When a professor holds the line on the breakpoint of what merits a passing grade, customer service is upheld. When a student is suspended due to failing grades, all other students and alumni (as customers) are served.

Unfortunately everything is tending to devolve to the lowest common denominator as universities fight to retain students. Academic standards are highly susceptible to a pervading malaise of the "customer is always right" attitude. As businesses know, customers aren't always right; not when they demean employees, are thoughtless and rude to other customers, show disrespect for capital plant and equipment, and demonstrate other similar behaviors as cretins rather than valued customers.

Each day over 1.5 million people make a purchase at Best Buy, a corporation widely known for retailing consumer electronics. Annual sales for Best Buy are $19.5 billion, the result of over 500 million customer visits each year. Best Buy is obviously doing something right as far as customer relations are concerned. There is, however, one little glitch in this success story. Best Buy's chief executive officer, Brad Anderson, claims that as many as 100 million of these visits each year are undesirable (McWilliams, 2004). As far as Best Buy is concerned, the firm would rather have these customers shop elsewhere.

According to Mr. Anderson, Best Buy attracts a large number of undesirable customers, people who "buy products, apply for rebates, return the purchases, then buy them back at returned-merchandise discounts. They load up on 'loss leaders,' severely discounted merchandise designed to boost store traffic, then flip the goods at a profit on eBay." In short, Best Buy, like many businesses, has concluded that the customer isn't always right, and in some circumstances the customer is patently wrong. These customers do not add value to Best Buy; they only take away from the company while failing to establish fair reciprocity.

As academic standards fall, the value of university degrees in the United States is also beginning to fall. This is a very dangerous trend in a global economy that is focused on invading markets through electronic modalities. As domestic degrees lose their luster customers will seek to fill this value-added vacuum with attractive alternatives. The rise of private degree mills is evidence enough about the capacity of the marketplace to sense vulnerability and then fill niches offering lucrative returns.

If competition isn't enough of a pressure to furrow the brows of academics, then they merely have to examine the attitudes and behaviors of high school graduates who ultimately become their students. The coming student cohorts are accustomed to checking boxes—going through the motions—rather than actually doing the job that's required. They are living a virtual reality. They observe images of what *attending* school implies and then act out their roles according to scripts they have learned in television, the movies, radio, DVDs, iPods, Wiis, Bluetooths, and MP3s.

Colleagues attest to a pervasive banality with which students approach the classroom and their education. Students seem to believe that if they just attend class on a somewhat regular basis— make the ultimate sacrifice of showing up—that this equates to passing performance. The attitude seems to be that attendance, not learning, should be the defining point for course credit. Students only study if they want to improve the grade they might receive. Earning a degree has become synonymous in their minds with showing up in person.

Media is largely to blame for this conundrum, although higher education has also contributed to the malady. The images of education that live large and fresh in the minds of an electronic, text-messaged, and Internet-connected generation suggest something quite different than the traditional images prior cohorts played out over the past decades. Educators have been forced into becoming entertainers because the electronic attention spans are so brief. If your delivery isn't scintillating and attention-grabbing, then the prospects are that you won't get your points across.

Mark Edmundson, professor of English at the University of Virginia, recently recounted his unwitting slip into entertaining rather than educating in his book *Why Read?* (Edmundson, 2004).

He posits that we have become a consumer culture and thus are far more comfortable in watching rather than doing. Television and other electronic media have inculcated the perception that it is cool to observe. As a result, students most treasure laid-back classroom environments where contentiousness never raises its ugly head. They have developed this preference by identifying with low-key television personalities whose calm and wise personas radiate the ultimate in coolness.

Edmundson goes on to relate his abject horror in discovering his metamorphosis into a television personality. Student teaching evaluations point proudly to his non-aggressive, laid-back, and cool delivery of course content. He was commended for humor and flexibility in viewpoints. Edmundson read between the lines and recoiled at the image they conveyed. He had become nothing more than just a reflection of electronic media. This was a wake-up call that motivated him to question how he taught and why—questions that more college professors need to consider rather than how they just play to student ratings.

Students seem to allocate only a certain number of hours toward their college education. They have full agendas. They carefully dole out precious hours to earning income for material consumption and entertainment as well as allocating time for personal and family interests. The thought seems to be that if a professor can't get the material across in the allotted classroom time, then he or she has failed. Students appear to believe that non-class time should be limited to reviewing previously presented material and *perhaps* reading textbooks. Papers and assorted homework are beyond the call of decency. But they have developed coping strategies for these impositions—Internet term paper outlets.

Results from the National Survey of Student Engagement (Hoover, 2004) of 163,000 freshmen indicate that 44 percent of all undergraduate students spend *ten hours or less* in studying for classes each week. For students on a fifteen-credit course load per semester, that is approximately forty minutes for every semester credit, or two hours per each three-credit course. Faculty members indicate that with a full course load, students should be studying more than twenty-five hours per week in preparing for class. Clearly it is difficult to allocate more than ten hours per week in preparing for classes if students are simultaneously working anywhere from twenty to forty hours while taking fifteen credit hours of classes (and planning on two hours of partying for every hour in class). Given these findings, where will students find the time to properly socialize?

Academia has devolved along with the perceptual standards adopted by students. Professors are very sensitive to the impact from requiring too much work outside of class. They are cognizant of when their delivery fails to meet the minimum entertainment threshold—perhaps a minimum set by the lowest MTV program, reality TV series, or worst (best?) Jerry Springer show. They know without a doubt when their class isn't seen as "mellow" or "cool" by students. Faculty members know all this because of their teaching evaluations. Course assessments are being used to bludgeon professors into meeting the low standards set by customers. It's all about student ratings.

When a professor receives low teaching ratings, the burden of proof that these ratings are bogus falls on the professor. You have to explain why the ratings do not reflect your poor performance when by comparison your colleagues' ratings are much higher. It doesn't matter that the students—customers—filling out the assessments failed to live up to their responsibilities. It only matters that you have low customer ratings, and the customers are always right.

This context has stimulated grade inflation in the mistaken belief that higher grades can uniformly guarantee higher teaching ratings. To some extent this argument holds true. Grading can have an impact on teaching effectiveness perceptions. However, students are very sophisticated customers. They are not so cynical that they think teaching evaluations are ignored by academic administrators. Perhaps they don't have great faith that their input will be reviewed by someone in a position of authority who will address poor instructor ratings. But they have faith in an electronic and virtual world, believing that eventually their input will catch up with the perpetrator they have endured all semester.

Grade inflation, student ratings of teachers' entertainment quotients, pampering engagement tactics to attract students at any cost, minimal class preparation, and myriad other indicators suggest that it's well past time for a change. Higher education needs sweeping reform to regain credibility. What universities could benefit from at this awkward time is a demonstration of tough love for customers. It's past time to inject some sensibility in the tower, to achieve a sensible balance in the equation of reciprocity between customers and institutions.

There are so many promising avenues for instituting compassionate, yet tough, customer love that they almost defy description. Following are merely a few suggestions to stimulate discussions by faculty, academic administrators, staff, and students about how universities can regain credibility. In the process, universities can re-create a focus on lifelong education and careers rather than just checking boxes to receive a degree and a good-paying job.

It's time to reset our grading base in higher education. Grade inflation has made a grade of B equivalent with performance formerly associated with a grade of D. Students have become so used to demonstrating such limited mastery of subjects in return for grades of A and B that anything less than a B is considered outright failure. A grade of B is even a slap in the face. Higher education has lost the bell-shaped curve where a C was considered average but entirely acceptable performance. Students now view a C as equivalent with an F, and perish the thought that they might actually receive a D.

There is one momentous change that can turn this situation around. Tough love means disconnecting (or connecting less) student teaching evaluations from annual salary increases. Professors can always benefit from customer input on ways to enhance and improve teaching, but universities must reconsider interpreting student evaluations as the single most meaningful measure of faculty teaching performance. This suggests that faculty and academic administrators should work harder in creating teaching performance portfolios—written student comments, peer class visits, instructional development, course innovations, and other multiple assessments of teaching effectiveness.

As long as professors know that the grades they give to students will impact their evaluation and ultimately their pay, grade inflation will prevail. In changing this scenario academic units can reward professors who maintain tough grading standards (as well as those who demonstrate exemplary performance on other teaching effectiveness measures). Yes, in many respects, it's that simple.

Tough love for customers also means revising our testing and evaluation processes. Unfortunately this implies work for professors. Even though finals are required at many of the universities I have served as a faculty member, seldom more than 20 percent of all classes actually give a final. I'm always amazed to discover that my colleagues and the vast majority of students have departed long before I administer finals. Undoubtedly there is a reverse halo effect on my teaching evaluations because I have the gall to administer a final.

In many academic programs, I have taught the senior capstone course. It's an eye-opening experience because I have a chance to see students just before they graduate. This is also a great opportunity to make observations about their writing and communication abilities as well as to assess their critical thinking skills. Often it is a pretty depressing realization that people will soon receive a college degree when they cannot communicate effectively in writing or lack the analytical ability to examine a table of data from which to draw meaningful conclusions.

However, I am especially amazed that so many students can negotiate a four-year degree with almost no term paper requirements or significant writing assignments. Increasingly the norm is so-called objective testing. Today students love objective tests filled with multiple choice questions and true-false answers. For professors it is a perfect strategy to minimize time invested in grading. For students, it is an approach consistent with limited command of course content. They do not have to master the material; they only need have a vague familiarity sufficient to guess among a few alternatives—skill that is cultivated early in their youth by computer games.

Frankly, I am certain that many of my more conscientious colleagues are tired of seeing their peers award a grade of B if students dutifully show up to class and a grade of A if they make the herculean effort to complete a paper. We are angry when another professor assigns blanket A's while differentiating with plusses and minuses. I once taught a course back-to-back with a technology management class in our Executive MBA program. Finals were scheduled for the following Friday and (in my case) Saturday. On Wednesday, I made the mistake of using the copy machine. My counterpart, who should be administering a final on Friday, had inadvertently left the grade sheet for his class on the copy machine. There would be no final. He had already assigned all A's. Justice did prevail; this was the last time he ever taught in the program.

Tough love for customers means giving students what they pay for—full-time core faculty who maintain vibrant teaching, research, and service programs. Research informs teaching; research improves teaching and adds substantial value to students' education. I am convinced that those in the professorate maintain their intellectual vitality through research, and they pass on this quality to students. Consequently, if professors aren't actively involved in research, then by definition they essentially emulate programmed instruction—we can get machines to do this more effectively at lower cost.

Far too many universities are providing course coverage through full-time lecturers, graduate assistants, teaching assistants, and doctoral students. With all due respect to the highly capable and conscientious individuals who fall into this category, they enable universities to perpetuate fraud. Universities—especially the huge doctoral degree–granting public universities—advertise the high quality of their faculty members. After baiting students to enroll (due to their prestigious faculty), these same institutions then switch out full-time faculty in favor of doctoral students. By definition, doctoral students are still completing their course of study. Where is the commitment to a high quality education in this evasive tactic?

The well-known little secret about course coverage by full-time core faculty is the substitution phenomenon known as the "instructor of record." Universities schedule classes by assigning full-time faculty to provide coverage. This is the façade. In reality the assigned professor doesn't teach the course—that is, show up to every class and deliver course material to students—but rather serves as the titular authority (i.e., the instructor of record) behind the class. A graduate assistant, doctoral student, or lecturer performs the bulk of class contact. This facilitates reducing the professor's onerous teaching load while allowing him or her to focus on research.

Tough love for customers by universities means placing strict limits on students' programs of study. Expectations should be raised that students will complete their degrees in an expeditious manner. Four-year college degrees are a misnomer. Students are taking six years and longer to complete their degrees. Universities grant leniency for time toward degree completion by accommodating student work schedules. Historically non-traditional students were those who primarily worked and secondarily took classes each semester. Now, non-traditional students on most university campuses are those who study full-time.

Students argue that unless they work, they can't pay their bills. Do they mean school-related bills, or conspicuous consumption bills? That argument smacks of being a bit spurious for many who do not know true financial exigency. Where does it end? Does it make sense to allow eight years to complete a four-year degree given the decreasing half-life of knowledge? Of course, as universities increase their expectations for expedient degree completion they can expect to lose students to institutions that have already relaxed time requirements, such as the proprietary degree mills. Does this improve higher education in the long run if capable students are given the incentive to attend programs with less academic rigor?

These and related thorny problems surrounding degree completion stare higher education straight in the face. By lowering standards, we have dug a hole for ourselves that will be extremely difficult to claw out of as pressures mount to maintain enrollment for revenue's sake. Furthermore, lower standards have depreciated the price that many institutions can charge. They cannot charge a premium because their programs are not seen as adding sufficient value for the price. Only by rethinking their niches and aligning resources appropriately will universities be able to reverse the insidious downward spiral stimulated by lowering standards.

FACULTY

The final component of the internal customer triumvirate is faculty. Higher education needs to set more ambitious expectations for one internal customer in particular—faculty members. It's through faculty efforts to impart knowledge, values, skills, and thinking that universities add value to students. When seen in this light, it is obvious that faculty members are as important a customer to universities as students. Therefore, it is only appropriate to show tough love for faculty as it is for students.

Tough love for faculty implies no longer tolerating burnt-out, cynical, and sarcastic professors. As Pink Floyd so aptly put it, "We don't need dark sarcasm in the classroom." Universities can do much more in setting high expectations for professors and holding them accountable. Those that fail to meet high standards should be sent packing. It's a distinct honor to be a member of the professorate, but there are also standards of behavior and performance that professors should maintain to continue within the academy. Higher education can dramatically improve not only the standards but also the enforcement of these expectations.

Universities cannot tolerate faculty members who do not perform at the highest professional level because of the damage these professors do to their institutions' good name and reputation. Low-performing faculty members only chase off good students and make it difficult to attract high-quality prospective students. When this happens, the quality of alumni erodes and with it a potential base of resource support. As a result, there is clear and powerful incentive for universities to attract and retain only the best faculty and then to nurture them to encourage superlative performance.

Unfortunately exactly the opposite chain of events tends to occur. Mediocre and marginal faculty members inevitably seem to require more than their fair share of administrative attention and support resources. Often more resources are invested in maintaining mediocrity than in building excellence. Faculty members who challenge this paradigm by demonstrating superior performance or who aspire to rise above average performance may face impressive peer sanctions and subtle hazing. Like so many institutions, higher education tends to drive things toward the average—a norm of satisfactory, but not exemplary, performance.

A colleague at another university shared a story about their efforts to hire two systems faculty members. The school was short on tenure-track systems faculty. Although eyebrows were raised when the dean permitted the systems department to extend offers to two faculty members during the summer without input from other departments, consensus suggested that the school needed to make progress in this area to maintain accrediting standards for full-time faculty coverage.

Both new faculty members were senior assistant professors at their respective institutions. This is a euphemism for the reality that neither could make tenure at their home institution. So their respective moves gave them a new lease on professorial life. Still, the die was cast. They were in the lower quartile of their graduating classes in terms of results produced after graduation. Neither was a stellar teacher. Both balanced teaching mediocrity with remarkably uninspiring research.

One of the two new faculty members managed to raise his research performance sufficiently to overcome the tenure hurdle. Luckily, work completed at his former institution was accepted in two second-tier journals, and he coasted into tenure at his new affiliation on the slimmest of margins. The second was struggling from the moment he arrived. Lack of progress in research was exacerbated by outfall from miserable teaching in the classroom.

The assistant professor in question held a most presumptuous sense of superiority over students. He simply could not denigrate students enough for their lack of quantitative preparation throughout their education. In contrast, he was good, but not great, in massaging numbers. His classes focused on elaborate formulas and intricate mathematical derivations because he felt most comfortable in displaying his quantitative superiority to students.

Rather than helping students learn quantitative systems analysis, he assumed that their deficiencies proved their intellectual inferiority and validated his superiority. Students feared attending his class because he would randomly pick on a student and then ask questions guaranteed to make him or her seem ignorant. Rather than address common mistakes on home assignments by the class as a whole, he spent class time in tirades about how they were not studying enough and how pathetic their math training was compared to the few class leaders.

The predictable occurred. Within his first year, the assistant professor had motivated students to complain vociferously about his condescending attitudes. His cynicism about their skills was self-fulfilling as more students gave up rather than try to master the concepts. Even brilliant, mature students castigated the professor for his disdainful attitude.

Three years after hearing this story, I once again met the colleague who told this tale at another conference. After catching up on our lives, I asked him about the arrogant assistant professor. What was his status? The tale was not uncommon. He was mired in his assistant professorship. It appeared unlikely that the university would ever grant tenure to such a sarcastic, unhappy individual.

But, I asked, doesn't this mean that it will be years before his tenure case is heard and he finally receives a terminal contract?

By all calculations he will have abused students for at least seven years. My friend sighed and looked me straight in the eye. In the end it will cost the university less to award tenure than to take on the legal battle. His teaching has achieved marginality; his research, acceptability. Higher-ups won't stand behind a decision to deny tenure.

The point of this illustration is how little universities struggle to uphold high standards. They would rather abuse countless customers—students—than risk the short-run costs of an expensive trial. All sorts of rationales are used to claim that substandard performance is above average performance when it isn't. Students deserve better than this; they are worthy of an invigorating learning environment with professors who challenge them intellectually while simultaneously helping them overcome learning obstacles.

"Professors behaving badly as internal customers" is unfortunately a common malady when faculty members move into an administrative role. Bad behavior can often be significantly attenuated when faculty assume leadership positions that give them extensive authority beyond traditional faculty roles. Some of the most egregious cases of outright irresponsible behavior surface when professors strike out in what amounts to a chance to try their hand at administering colleagues and staff. In many cases, the intentions are sincere, but the execution of authority is misguided. In the worst case scenarios, power corrupts.

What is there about a promotion to an administrative title that adversely infects people, causing their brains and good sense to turn to mush? Whatever the causal factors, faculty members seem to have a special predilection for becoming petty bureaucrats. Perhaps this tendency is the result of trying too hard or the lack of competent role models. Certainly the lack of formal training and education in management contributes to poor performance. Most faculty members can patiently understand and work through these sub-par assignments with forgiving attitudes. But eventually, a tyrant acquires power and turns things topsy-turvy. These cases cry for tough love and even swifter action.

Early one morning I was bounding up the stairs toward my beloved office intent on catching at least two hours of undisturbed bliss in writing the initial paragraphs on a research article for a mid-level refereed journal. My mind was spinning already with the initial critical paragraph and a precise hook to capture the reviewers' attention. Write one good paragraph and the remainder of the manuscript would flow like wine from a bottomless carafe. Two different approaches were being weighed as I scaled those last few steps and then my heart sank.

At the top of the veranda in dawn's dusky shadows was the unmistakable full figure of a senior colleague. He was cloaked in a gossamer veil of soft light and humidity—for once we had received a long-needed theatrical thunderstorm the preceding night that filled the air with precious water vapor. I had been reveling in the aromas of a fresh day with its implications for a tsunami of creative thinking that shortly would be injected full strength into my latest intellectual contribution for the year. Suddenly that vision seemed perilously tenuous. In a spilt second, I realized that my constructive morning was about to be blasted to smithereens by a meddling sour professor who was intent on controlling everything that happened in our department.

As I topped out on the crumbling concrete veranda, his wraithlike apparition seemed to blossom (or perhaps he had managed to put on another ten pounds since I last saw him). Whatever the explanation, his insidious bulk reached out to tackle me the moment my first foot hit that highest-most deck.

"Howard, I'm glad to see you and happy that I caught you this morning before you began to prepare for class."

This was a little dig on his part. He was more than slightly jealous of my publishing productivity, and he knew that I wasn't coming in this early to arrange my next modest class lecture. His sarcasm didn't incite a reaction because I knew very well that I could out-teach him any day. Our students had informed me over the years that he maintained a cool distance and self-righteous attitude. He unequivocally knew best, and his opinion on all class subjects was unapproachable—if you wanted to pass his class. Even the most mindless students figured this out quickly and simply spit back his opinions on midterm short essay questions or during class discussions. They only needed to think exactly like him to receive an "A" for the course.

"Well Frank, I am surprised to see you here so early. You here for a meeting with the dean?"

Two can play that passive-aggressive game. My comment underscored that he seldom came in before 10:00 A.M.—one must have his coffee and read the morning's newspaper after all—and that he was an unabashed brownnoser always poised to tell the dean how great a job she was doing and then slyly (and sometimes not so cleverly) telling her how she could better manage our college. Of course, he phrased his sentiments and proclamations in such a constructive fashion that our poor low-GMAT dean never saw how she was being ridiculed. She was oblivious to the obvious.

"No. I'd like to spend a few minutes if you have the time."

"If you have the time." That euphemistic phrase can be translated as "I'm going to use up whatever productive time you have set aside this morning." I knew that I should have gone out for a little field research this morning—my code name for exercise.

We wove through the halls and entered into my musty but tidy office. There is sufficient enough space for one visitor, but his physical presence more than fleshed out the room. It was his personality that ultimately strangled me, and claustrophobia began to wheedle its way into my mind. He closed the door with a thud.

"I'm so happy to catch you, and I will be very brief. I'm here to take a reading on your thoughts about our department chair. How do you think she is doing after six months under our new dean?"

So that's the issue—the public lynching of our department chair is about to take place. By his indomitable presence and razor sharp inquiry, I now knew all that I needed to know, and more, about this little benign visit by one of my beloved and highly esteemed colleagues.

I waited for him to answer the question for me.

Surely he didn't want my opinion or value what I really thought. He was here to tell me exactly what I should be thinking. Like a dutiful Labrador retriever, I remained in my chair wagging my tail with my tongue hanging out of my mouth.

Fifteen seconds went by.

Silence filled the room.

I've learned to keep my mouth shut in these situations. Eventually the other person will feel compelled to fill the echoing silence with words. There's absolutely no reason to tip my hand at this point—that might give him some additional advantage. Besides his shallowness was well known to me and him. This moment had been carefully orchestrated and well rehearsed. All I was expected to do is patiently wait for him to begin.

"I don't know if you've noticed that our department chair has gone over to the Dark Side?" He was referring, of course, to a major philosophical difference between him and our dean. In truth he was right. Our department chair had become the dean's perfect little toady.

"Uhh. . . hah." was all that escaped from my parched lips before he launched back into his feigned soliloquy.

"A number of us in the department are thinking that a change in leadership may be necessary before too much damage is done with the forthcoming annual performance evaluations."

My own meager raise flashed before my eyes as I contemplated being caught between two faculty members behaving badly— him, my colleague and her, my colleague-turned-rogue-administrator."

In fact he had a very good point. Several of my colleagues insinuated that our department chair had turned out to be a viciously vindictive Neanderthal. What a shame this transformation had occurred. She was a good, but not great, scholar. She had a reputation as an entertaining lecturer—there was little-to-no discussion in her classes because it was all about her biased liberal opinion on every subject. Rumor had it that she would browbeat any student who dared to confront her with an opposing view. Plenty of evidence from collegial testimony existed suggesting this was more than rumor.

Ten years earlier I had turned on the television one evening to catch up on the news. There on the tube was a political debate. My colleague was one of three candidates running for office. At that time the issue of legalizing marijuana was captivating our community. When the moderator asked my colleague about her position, she puffed out her chest and stanchly defended legalization of marijuana. What happened next was astounding—the only time I had seen someone put my colleague in her place.

The moderator asked the next candidate what he thought about my colleague's stance. The candidate replied in a concise phrase, "That was the most irresponsible thing I have ever heard in my life."

End of point.

End of debate.

End of my colleague's political aspirations.

Not only did my department chair smother her colleagues with her one-sided opinions, she began to get back at everyone for any little slight or disagreement they may have had with her over the years. Impeccable research records were assessed as not having quality (in the eyes of the department chair). One negative student comment and she concluded that a professor was an abject failure in the classroom. Raises were given out with almost complete disregard for rational criteria other than the whims of the chair. Summer research funds were summarily cut by half and weirdly reallocated to young faculty who had not produced despite being highly supported for four or five years.

But more than these offenses, the department chair had a well-earned reputation among faculty for teaching bias. No wonder my colleague was visiting this early morning. He had been a victim of this harassment. The pendulum was about to swing the other direction because people had suffered enough.

How sad to see a formerly respected colleague fall so quickly from grace. We all knew her motivations and experienced her tyranny. Egged on by the dean, our department chair managed to turn her department completely on end. Colleagues suddenly stopped socializing with her. She roamed the halls looking for a bit of friendly banter, but no one was home. She had scared everyone into going to ground.

One afternoon I walked by her office. The door was slightly ajar and there she sat all by herself. No students. No colleagues. No body. What a disappointing way to end what had otherwise been a respectable career. Her legacy would forever be her bullying tactics and vindictive retaliation. After all of those years and countless students, she faded into oblivion. My colleagues had dished out a whopping dose of tough love. They replaced her without as much as a five-minute discussion. A new candidate was nominated and summarily forwarded to the dean.

Despite a few faculty members who shirk their professorial responsibilities, the rest of my colleagues strive hard to fulfill their responsibilities. These are decent, hard-working professionals who are very committed to higher education and the students they serve. Occasionally they slip up and need a bit of tough love. But for the most part, I have found that university faculty members sacrifice way beyond the remuneration they receive for performing their duties.

What greater statement about a colleague's character can be made than the case where self-sacrifice led to a posthumous publication for another friend? In this case, our colleague had carefully taken a manuscript through submission, revision, re-review, and resubmission to his field's leading journal. Alas, he passed away from cancer before the manuscript was published. The editor still was waiting for him to put finishing touches on several revisions demanded by the reviewers.

In stepped another colleague who addressed each of the reviewers' concerns and responded to the additional expectations of the editor. This colleague did not put his name on the manuscript. *He did it out of respect for his colleague.* Can you imagine that? He took away from his own research publication agenda to make certain the article was published and his departed colleague received full credit. That's quite a sacrifice.

I think about another young assistant professor who could not offer more help to his students. He held review sessions throughout the weeks leading to each exam. He was perpetually in his office, door wide open and waiting patiently for an inquiring mind to show up. For all we knew, he only went home on weekends. You can only imagine how laudatory his teaching evaluations were. They sparkled with gratitude from students who could not quite grasp the course content until my colleague turned on the light bulb for them.

Another colleague was always—every single time—willing to help a community request for assistance. He made my job so much easier. All I had to do was pick up the phone and call Pat whenever I fielded a call from the community for assistance. I gave him the details and asked him to contact the client. Every time he followed up within twenty-four hours. I realized that this was simply the way he did business—it was a personal signature about his professorship.

In sum, before becoming too jaded about the motivations of faculty members and their need for tough love, let's remember the hard-working women and men who each and every single day perform with the highest standards in mind. As far as faculty is concerned, it's more the exception than the rule that is at play here. Academics enter the profession because they love learning and teaching. They tend to be self-motivating. However, everyone can fall off the cart. People change over their careers. Administrators do stupid things that incite adverse reactions. Personal circumstances change. Save tough love for the exceptions and your university will be richly rewarded in the process.

In the final analysis, professors need tough love too. When universities lower expectations for faculty members, they only encourage the sort of behavior and performance that is antithetical to such a noble profession. Professors, students, and alumni exist in a self-supporting synergy. When any one element is deficient, the others suffer. Thus, it behooves institutions of higher education to demonstrate tough love across the board. But professors especially need tough love as they occupy positions to influence impressionable minds. They determine the balance of the relationship between alumni and university as years roll by.

Chapter 9

TAKING BACK THE
IVORY TOWER

A compelling imperative exists to rescue higher education from its long-running stupor. Costs have progressively escalated over the decades while value has diminished. Many taxpayers perceive education to be a sinkhole for their dollars. More money is poured in, yet there never seems to be an end to the insatiable demand. Universities and colleges resemble bloated bureaucracies where costs go unchecked, academic standards have dissipated, spoiled professors play childish games, and leadership is nonexistent. All that investment in higher education doesn't seem to be improving our society or its ability to compete in a global economy.

It's time for a change. It's time to take back the tower and regain sanity on college campuses. *Taking Back the Tower* prescribes six commonsense ideas for solving critical problems confronting our colleges and universities. These ideas are not suggested as a panacea but rather a logical approach that will accomplish the most good. Every university situation differs, and thus this repertoire for suggested change should be adjusted accordingly. The key idea is to focus on a few strategic changes that lead to the highest impact.

Above all, as suggested by this book's prelude, we want to encourage constructive evolution while avoiding revolution. There is so much less to be gained from revolution. Universities require prudent overhaul, not destruction. Nonetheless, some of the ideas proposed in *Taking Back the Tower* will be seen by faculty members as tantamount to revolution, and they will galvanize forces accordingly to fight the good fight in the name of perpetuating mediocrity.

No; we don't want or need revolution to effect the changes that will resurrect universities and return them as an icon of public admiration. Instead, constructive evolution implies systematic and comprehensive improvement. Universities can vitally benefit from continuous improvement. But at the same time, a level of urgency exists that obviates the academic timeframe. We no longer have the luxury of time. Taxpayers expect relief now. Society demands a far greater return on the resources invested in all entities receiving governmental funds (in whole or part; public university or private university). Thus, the plodding, incremental approach to doing things the academic way must be discarded for agile and timely actions.

An unanswered question is who will lead this effort to take back the ivory tower? We're talking here about a fundamental shaking of universities to their very core. This implies widespread consternation and ambiguity, an environment that occasionally cycles between chaos and managed agitation. This does not imply a fun context filled with good times, and it is certainly not the sort of environment that leads to healthy learning or seminal scholarship. But short-run costs will be more than justified by the long-run gains. Such a disrupted environment calls for leaders who possess considerable fortitude, foresight, and commitment to see a difficult period of change through to its end.

WHO WILL LEAD CONSTRUCTIVE EVOLUTION?

A quick appraisal of the university community confirms that leadership for constructive evolution probably won't surface within institutions of higher education. This is disappointingly sad, but true. If we look carefully at the major players, other than students, there are more disincentives than there are incentives to emerge internally as leader.

It is critical to acknowledge that many admirable leaders can be found in higher education. I have been lucky to serve under a few of them and their contribution is impressive; their mentoring impeccable. Sadly, they are the exception rather than the rule.

On the face of it, faculty members will not lead a constructive evolution because they have it so good under the current system. They don't want change because it will mean reducing their perquisites and possibly cutting into their undesignated time to complete research, to prepare for classes, and to behave like faculty. They much prefer to sit on the sidelines and occasionally come out of their shells to take potshots at others who are trying to accomplish something worthwhile. Leadership means that they leave themselves open to criticism; they would much rather criticize than be criticized.

Department chairs will not lead the constructive evolution because they are only short-time administrators who are not paid sufficiently to take on the risks associated with leading change. Chairs think more like faculty than administrators. As a result, they persistently side with faculty because department chairs are most often elected to their positions. Furthermore, chairs typically rotate back onto the faculty after completing their terms—usually something on the order of every four years. Thus, chairs have neither the financial nor professional incentives to lead evolutionary change.

Deans could lead constructive evolution, but there are too many disincentives to lead the charge, and the risk is too high that any individual dean, or deans, will find themselves out on the edge without support from above. Unless constructive evolution is orchestrated by the provost in a concerted, organized, and formal manner, any dean runs the risk of losing support from faculty. If a dean initiates change within her or his college without the provost's approval, that dean is left with great exposure. The provost may be disinclined to support the dean when faculty members pummel the provost with protests.

The dean who acts like a lone wolf is asking for trouble. Although deans' intentions at instituting evolutionary change within their units may appear to be admirable, unless the effort is part of a campus-wide initiative, faculty will question why their college is undergoing such change while others on campus adhere to the status quo. Their predictable reaction is a vote of no confidence, which opens the door for provost discretion. Moreover, renegade deans (who unilaterally attempt to transform their units) must crave punishment because even with the provost's support, he or she will face tumultuous internal battles that sap energy and morale.

In most instances, we cannot count on provosts to lead constructive evolution because many are too busy posturing to assume a presidency somewhere. You cannot become president if you have an angry faculty on campus that will inform other institutions about what they perceive to be a lack of academic leadership. Provosts generally want a happy status quo. They may tinker with a few changes, and they may initiate campus-wide initiatives that ultimately lead to making no meaningful decisions, but they typically do not have the incentive to lead constructive evolution. They just want to bide their time and have everyone in high spirits until their presidency calls.

Presidents occupy a favored position for leading constructive evolution, but in the final analysis, they tend to live down to our expectations for leadership. Universities are massive organizations that are difficult to steer. They are not like huge corporations where directives are issued and there is a high probability that these directives will be obeyed or else. Presidents have a board of trustees, or regents, to appease (like corporations). But presidents generally cannot summarily dismiss faculty if they refuse to follow their leadership. Universities function through collegial governance. This dilutes presidential power.

Presidents are too busy addressing a vast continuum of constituents to risk constructive evolution that might morph into revolution. They occupy the frustrating position of having to rely entirely on others to get the job done. Unfortunately this means that they are continually dragged down into current operating issues—unexpected higher utility costs, alumni distress over the football team's performance, student demonstrations over a professor's unpatriotic slur in class, and other unanticipated perturbations—and forced to leave big picture issues behind. Given all of the many constituents they are trying to satisfy and the vast continuum of issues they have to address, presidents easily slip into a mode of satisficing; that is, making the most out of the status quo. Not coincidentally, this is the same mindset held by provosts, their right-hand confidant.

Regents and trustees, like presidents, are in a position to implement significant change in universities, but they seldom have the incentives or know-how for achieving this end. Regents tend to be political appointments, especially in public institutions of higher education. They may have very limited knowledge of how universities run, but out of the goodness of their hearts they serve because they see that universities vitally need change. Trustees in private universities are less susceptible to political appointment, but another insidious motive brings the wrong people to these boards. Wealthy alumni who potentially can enrich their alma mater are incorporated on boards of trustees with one goal in mind, and that isn't leading academic change—it's giving money.

In view of the large scale of university operations, regents and trustees can only achieve a superficial understanding of how a university functions, where weaknesses exist, and how change might be implemented. Since regents tend to meet on an infrequent basis, they can only address so many problems. Most are not paid; these are people with vibrant, active lives, otherwise they never would have risen to the position in the first place. Additionally, they are dependent on the president to feed them information. Presidents act as gatekeepers on what regents or trustees know about where an institution has been, what information they receive on where an institution is headed, and what few problems (from a vast array) they will tackle.

Looking within universities, it is apparent why leadership for constructive evolution has never surfaced. People either do not have the incentive, the time, the authority or support of higher authority, or the knowledge base to lead sweeping change. In fact, prevailing incentives motivate people to act like barbarians. Having taken over the ivory towers, they are very reticent to relinquish control because it's such a good life cloistered within those hallowed halls whether you are faculty, academic administrator, or trustee.

All is not lost; however. Taxpayers and their representatives— legislators—are fully prepared to lead constructive change. They certainly have the incentive to pressure ivory towers into cleaning up their act. The public has grown weary of spending so much for so little. Taxpayers and legislators hear about faculty high jinks— admittedly only a few bad apples spoiling the whole bunch—and they know in their hearts that they can't get away with such antics, in such luxury, where they work. Moreover, taxpayers are tired of working hard to earn their dollars and then watching them be frittered away by people and institutions that should know better.

Already legislators and taxpayers are seeking greater accountability from higher education. Crude report cards are being put into practice in some states under the rubric of accountability. This is a good intention, but its implementation is quite slow. Much time is being consumed in defining measures and how data will be collected before being condensed into meaningful reports. Furthermore, these unsophisticated reports cannot capture the breadth and depth of outcomes produced by universities, much less the vast range of their activities and programs.

Academics are quick to criticize the assessment methodologies legislators and governmental commissions are using to evaluate resource use. Unfortunately academics are focusing on the wrong thing. They should be encouraging extensive discourse about the implications of external pressures. Instead they dwell on what measures are being used and how accurate the data are that comprise reports.

In short, staring the academic community in the face is an opportunity to maintain self-control versus losing control to external parties like legislatures and governmental commissions. But universities seem loathe to take action. Often it takes a good whack in the head before you can change someone's thinking and behavior. Apparently this is also the case for institutions of higher education.

WHO SHOULD TAKE THE LEAD?

Given that universities continue to muddle along and legislatures are implementing annual assessments with glacial speed, an opportunity still exists for someone to rise to the occasion in taking back the tower. With a few exceptions, most universities are in the same boat of battling stiff economic reform associated with financial market failures, energy constraints, global competition, and fallout from terrorism. But universities are not so destitute that the populace is parading down the streets burning faculty in effigy and taking over presidents' offices in an impassioned call for revolution.

I believe that **the appropriate leader for constructive academic evolution should be the professorate.** Universities would make substantial progress toward responsible stewardship if faculty members stepped up to lead their institutions. Faculty have all the right incentives and the know-how to institute progressive, yet lasting, changes that are in the best interests of students and scholarship. But few campuses will see their core faculties rise to the occasion and demonstrate the leadership that is so desperately needed.

Faculty members have a governance structure that ensures representation and leadership in managing wide scale reform—the faculty senate. I'll wait a minute while my academic friends stop rolling on the floor in laughter.

There—do they feel better now? I know how absurd this suggestion sounds. At virtually every university at which I have served as a faculty member, there exists a quaint body known as the faculty senate. From what I and my colleagues can ascertain, the chief role and results of the faculty senate are to complain. We want more in raises. We want a better faculty club. We admonish dean so-and-so for taking away faculty prerogative. We think the athletics program is receiving too much money. And, so the faculty senate goes in the collective mind of those who aren't senate representatives. Faculty senators are essentially a sample of faculty members skewed with an overrepresentation of blowhards that make no discernible contribution other than obstructing progress.

In truth many well meaning women and men assume the additional burden of an assignment to the faculty senate. They make every attempt to do a conscientious job of representing their colleges and colleagues. Unfortunately there are too many opportunities for embittered peers to occupy these important governance positions. These professional grousers can waste others' valuable time in their efforts to embarrass university administrators or to prove a specious point.

Think how powerful the faculty and faculty senate could become if the professorate collectively agrees that it will *lead constructive evolution*? Faculty members have so much to lose if leadership is relinquished to academic administrators, regents, legislatures, or public commissions. Imagine how the public would react favorably to a world in which vastly privileged faculty members actually use their awesome brain power to solve problems in their own institutions (instead of telling other people and organizations how to solve their problems). It would be a startling revelation and most refreshing.

Well, the prospects for faculty leading the charge are not good. External pressures will likely prevail and gradually instill sanity in the ivory towers. In some universities, the arguments put forth in *Taking Back the Tower* will be heard and taken to heart. Leadership will emerge from some source—a president with fire in the belly, a provost who seriously takes responsibility for earning his or her salary, or regents who cannot stand the wishy-washy answers they continue to receive whenever they put the president on the spot.

In the few enlightened institutions of higher education that are ready to move forward with constructive evolution, *Taking Back the Tower* offers a template for initiating change. Let's turn to implementation issues associated with commonsense solutions for saving higher education.

AN INVERTED PYRAMID FOR CHANGE

What is the best way to go about implementing the ideas shared in this book? This is an inevitable question for those who are intent on helping universities claw their way back to respectability. Unfortunately there is no one best way; proper implementation is contingent on the specific setting. The commonsense solutions proffered in *Taking Back the Tower* merely reflect what the typical university should consider to extract the most gain with the least pain. But any single strategy for reform depends on relevant variables in a specific university setting. For example, if a university has already honed its strategic plan, then it should proceed immediately to implementation and turn to other commonsense solutions for effectuating change.

For institutions in which almost no discernible progress has been made toward effective management of resources, Figure 9.1 presents an inverted pyramid of priorities to consider. Three phases

Figure 9.1. Inverted Pyramid of Priorities for Saving Higher Education

are defined that unfold over a three-year period. As this figure suggests, leadership through strategic management is the foundation upon which other change strategies rest.

PHASE ONE

If you don't know where you're going and you don't care in which direction you are going, then any old path will suffice. Such journeys can be filled with excitement and be very rewarding in terms of what's received from your effort. Unfortunately, this is no way to run a university. Substantial resources are at stake as well as significant impacts on people's lives. A random saunter through the woods is not an appropriate way to lead a university. Perhaps more than ever, leadership in strategic management is the foremost challenge to those in the top echelons of our colleges and universities.

Strategic management is the cornerstone to taking the ivory tower back. The strategic management process (Chapter 3) defines a vision of what a university should strive to become as well as explaining (through its mission) what this university is and what it tries to accomplish. Above all in these trying financial times, strategic leadership helps universities define what they are not, that is, what academic programs they do not offer. Knowing what you do not do—the academic programs a university doesn't offer nor will attempt to offer—is just as valuable as clearly understanding what you do best.

Universities particularly need a crystal clear focus to ensure that resources are deployed to their highest and best use. Given the growing scarcity of public funding for higher education, it's past time for universities to focus resources on their leading programs— those initiatives for which they are distinctive—rather than squandering resources across a broad array of mediocre efforts. Focus has become an imperative driving the intelligent management of valuable university assets and operating funds.

As Figure 9.1 suggests, all other commonsense solutions to problems in higher education rest on a solid foundation of strategic management. University strategic plans provide a road map spelling out their intended directions. These plans also establish objectives against which progress can be compared In short, strategic management helps to control present performance while guiding efforts toward the future. A framework is created defining logically how resources are to be spent (or not expended) and how performance is assessed. This facilitates necessary adjustments to accomplish objectives, mission, and vision.

In terms of time frame for taking back the tower, one year is suggested for attaining leadership in strategic management. I can just see the academic heads wagging now, indicating that this is far too ambitious a time frame. Megacorporations with billions of dollars in assets and thousands of employees have been forced by market pressures to become very agile in revising their strategic plans and in implementing revisions. Why do universities think that they are so special that they cannot possibly complete such a process in less than one year?

Most universities already have strategic plans. What they need to do is whip them into shape and begin deploying them in daily decision-making. It is possible to review and revise strategic plans in a short period of time while soliciting extensive feedback from key stakeholders. It is possible to use this process to narrow the focus of a university's academic programs. However, none of this will be accomplished without assertive leadership. Whoever leads the planning process—regents, president, provost, or committee (e.g., faculty senate leaders plus academic administrators)—must ensure that the time frame is understood, that opportunities abound for input, and that focusing the plan is paramount. Then these leaders must lead by making tough decisions.

PHASE TWO

The inverted pyramid in Figure 9.1 indicates that a second layer of initiatives exists relative to taking back the ivory tower. With strategic management firmly guiding these next steps, universities should move toward ensuring the highest and best use of resources and aligning incentives with reality. Aided by a freshly reviewed and reaffirmed strategic plan, universities can then instill some intelligence in their budgeting processes. Having narrowed the focus of what they are trying to accomplish, the budgeting process can begin to function with greater effectiveness in identifying resources to be reallocated and reinvested in light of the

strategic plan. Here is the opportunity to instill the decision criterion (and attitude) of highest and best use. Suddenly things begin
to fall into place.

A strategic plan spells out the intended direction, goals, and academic programs that a university aspires to achieve. Budgeting is
guided by a plan and enables resource allocations to be viewed in a
new light. Instead of budgeting according to the status quo, leaders
use the criterion of highest and best use (as guided by the strategic
plan). It only takes one budgeting cycle—a single iteration—to
launch this new mindset. Successive cycles will continue to draw
out better investments of existing resources.

In addition to pursuing highest and best resource use, universities can begin to align incentives with reality. Simply by entering
into multiyear contracts (with new faculty destined to become core
faculty) rather than making tenure commitments, a compelling
message is sent across campus that a new day has dawned relative
to professional expectations of faculty and staff. As new faculty
members are hired on multiyear contracts (rather than life
sentences), they will perform quite differently—more in synch
with a university's strategic direction—than existing faculty. In fact,
their behavior may well encourage many existing tenured or tenure
track faculty members to reassess how they have been performing.
Gradually, but within two to three years, the professorate
will exhibit more university-friendly and performance-oriented
attitudes, enabling their institution to progress toward greater
distinction.

It is the implied option not taken that correctly aligns behavior
and performance by tenured faculty with university aspirations. If
a university is awarding multiyear contracts to new faculty, then it
also has the option of revoking tenure from existing faculty in times
of financial exigency. Tenured faculty members intuitively understand this causal chain and the implied bond of an option not
taken.

In terms of time frame, Figure 9.1 suggests that instilling a policy
of highest and best use should begin in year two, when the strategic
plan is in place and its implementation has begun. Highest and
best use becomes the leading decision criterion associated with executing the strategic plan and budgeting in year two. The move to
align incentives with reality—ostensibly ending the awarding of
tenure—can also wait until the second year of taking back the tower.

Why muddy the waters surrounding strategic planning revisions by introducing the emotion of tenure issues?

Phase Three

The third phase of taking back the ivory tower begins in year three. By this point, sufficient time has elapsed relative to strategic planning (specifically objective setting at operating levels) that performance accountability unfolds with astonishing rigor. Faculty, staff, students, and academic administrators should be held accountable for their performance. Enough time has elapsed during year two for them to have honed their performance objectives. When annual performance reviews are undertaken in year three, it is time to hold people accountable for their performance.

This third phase also initiates efforts at tough love for internal and external customers. A university should be raising performance expectations and standards across the board for alumni, students, faculty, and staff commensurate with its strategic plan. By this point the entire university community should understand where the institution is headed because results of strategic planning and its execution have been effectively communicated.

The most shocking revelation will be that a university is actually following through with its strategic plan instead of just talking about it. Momentum begins to build toward continuous improvement in raising standards and expectations. Tough love melds into an entirely different way of thinking, behaving, and performing at the university.

In phase three, the culture of the university begins to clear. People—students, alumni, faculty, staff, administrators, trustees—are now on the same page. They hold the same values and expectations regarding the university. Philosophically they mesh relative to how the university functions while agreeing on the fundamental direction it is headed. Instead of fighting each other, cooperation and enhanced reciprocity flourish. Pride resurfaces in what the university stands for. Formerly unattainable goals are now seem as feasible. A distinct sense of what it means to be a student or graduate, faculty, or staff member begins to prevail. Cynicism and sarcasm evaporate. In short, a strategy supportive culture takes root and is progressively reinforced by performance.

In reality, implementation of commonsense solutions for saving higher education will not unfold as neatly or methodically as suggested by Figure 9.1. But we have a template conveying what an ideal model looks like. To be certain, applications of Figure 9.1 will have to be adjusted for specific considerations in each university setting. Perhaps strategic planning is already finely honed and it is just a matter of actually implementing the plan. In other cases, performance evaluations have never been rigorously applied and more time will be needed in this area.

What matters most is that institutions make rapid progress toward implementing the building blocks shown in Figure 9.1. In this manner, universities can anticipate self-healing and guard against external intervention or control. But more important, they will begin to raise higher education to a level hitherto unattained.

SENSITIVITY IN TAKING BACK THE TOWER

There is both an art and science to managing that, when combined, leads to the accomplishment of seemingly impossible dreams. Louis V. Gersner Jr. pulled off a miraculous turnaround of IBM through penetrating market analysis balanced with insightful leadership. Jack Welch increased the value of General Electric stock by $400 billion through savvy people management and establishing rigorous control of operations. The success of these business leaders and others wasn't merely a matter of good luck. They were very careful to attend to the fine details of how they went about implementing change.

It isn't enough to articulate a great idea or strategy. Execution is the other mysterious half of the equation. And so it is with efforts to take back the tower. If a university blindly adopted the principles outlined in this book, the intended goal of instilling sanity in operations and strategic direction still may not be achieved. The principles are important, but so too is the manner in which they are implemented. Strategies covered in the pages of *Taking Back the Tower* are most valuable when executed with sensitivity to both the culture that is being left behind and the future toward which a university is building.

Some years ago I was communicating with a dean at a university in the Rocky Mountains. We had co-authored a number of journal publications over the years and were thinking about collaborating on a book. In the course of several weeks we traded a prospectus back and forth, adding a chapter here while modifying a chapter there. We invested considerable attention to defining the target market and estimating its size. Then we put our heads together in devising marketing strategies that would get this book into the hands of our intended audience.

While I put finishing touches on the prospectus, my colleague was responsible for meeting the executive director of his university's press to ascertain interest in publishing our proposed book. University presses play a very significant role in disseminating academic contributions. In many cases, important scholarly books are not able to provide evidence of a large potential market or robust market penetration; for these books the intended audience is quite small. Large proprietary publishing houses are not interested in esoteric research or important contributions to literature unless there is considerable money to be made from selling lots of books. In contrast, university presses are agile and able to reach primarily regional markets that the big publishers miss. By publishing faculty scholarship, they extend the reputation of their universities (but unlike large publishers, struggle to break even).

I didn't hear from my colleague after his scheduled appointment with the executive director, so I gave him a call. He indicated that his meeting had been postponed for a week due to a crisis at the press. No big deal, it only gave me some more time to play with the prospectus. The following week, I was buried deep in drafting a chapter when the phone roused me from a stupor of intense concentration. The story my friend shared was simultaneously hysterically funny and pathetic. It served as a perfect illustration of an abysmal failure to properly execute strategy, thereby putting one of his university's most important academic contributions at high risk.

My colleague's first lunch with the director was postponed due to a managerial faux pas of the worst kind. A new president had recently taken the reins of the languishing institution. After fumbling about for several months, this new president embarked on an aggressive course of centralizing decision-making and streamlining business practices. In many respects this university, like so many others, could use a fresh approach in its operations. Unfortunately, the new president only knew the jargon of intelligent business management and absolutely nothing about the concepts or their implementation. His rhetoric sounded good but was sorely lacking when the rubber met the road.

My friend had already regaled me over the past months with tasty tidbits of ineffectual attempts by the new president to put his administrative team in place. The number of top administrators had doubled while results produced from this investment decreased inversely. The running joke on his campus was the fact that twice as many administrators were now needed to get half the amount of work done. It now took two people to screw in a light bulb.

However, a not-so-funny side accompanied this reorganization. A distressing authoritarianism replaced the university's collegial approach to managing. Operations management became a bit more efficient in some respects, but at the cost of dignified human relations. Above all, you didn't publicly express any criticism about university management even if in the best of intentions. The president and his henchmen only wanted to be surrounded by "yes-men."

Thus on the day that my colleague was to meet with the university press's executive director, a vice president for business operations (also new to the job) sent a much lower level minion over to deliver some bad news. The vice president wanted the building space in which the university press was housed. He had unilaterally decided to move the university press without conferring with the executive director. The unfortunate messenger was young and naive but resolutely loyal to the powers that be. He fumbled big time in delivering his message to the executive director.

The executive director was insulted and rightfully so. This university's press was one of its academic jewels. It wasn't just another part of business operations, a part of business as usual. The president and vice president didn't quite get it because of their arrogance and lack of academic experience. The press was part of the very academic fabric that distinguished this university. Treating it like just another business unit reflected their ignorance and disdain for anything academic—a bizarre attitude for those charged with managing an institution of higher learning.

By the time my co-author had lunch with the press's executive director, the crisis was over. A seasoned veteran, the director didn't waste his time on the minion but went straight to the top. In the process, he extricated wonderful physical facilities for his unit's operations that were located a pleasant distance from the depressing chaos on main campus. The director had also used this fumble by top management to elegantly inform them about the press's importance to the university. This administration too would pass, and pass very quickly at that, before a refreshing breath of fresh air returned the campus to a civilized, well-managed, and nurturing scholarly environment. It was just a matter of hunkering down and fulfilling the press's important mission.

My colleague shared a valuable insight from lunch with the seasoned executive director. The meeting was a smash as far as our prospectus was concerned. The press would consider it on the basis of merit, and it was now up to us to deliver a high quality manuscript. However, lunch provided much more than a door opening to the submission of a prospectus. My colleague came away with a crystal clear understanding of the big picture—of a university campus in crisis because the very topmost managers were mishandling their execution of change.

As we take back our ivory towers and instill some sanity let us not forget that the means—the principles espoused in this book—are as important as the end. Executing change should be accomplished in a manner worthy of our goal—enlightened institutions of higher education. Thus, the principles in *Taking Back the Tower* deserve to be implemented in ways that are consistent with the lofty goals and missions of our academic institutions. These aren't business practices that should be applied in a rote detached manner to achieve a predictable outcome. Effective strategy never blindly follows a precise formula during implementation; it also requires prudent judgment and sensitivity to the past culture.

In reformulating our institutions, we should never lose sight of the elusive concept of soul—that distinctive, but difficult to articulate, spiritual sense that differentiates universities. The last thing we want is to transform our centers of higher learning into machines that just churn out indistinguishable graduates and intellectual contributions. Instead we should aspire to improve how our universities function so that we enhance their distinctive spiritual qualities.

To lose the unique redeeming spirit of a university in the name of more efficient management would be a terrible crime. We want to make better use of the resources invested in universities without losing their distinctive characteristics. In fact, the intention of the principles suggested in this book is to increase the opportunities and wherewithal to build distinctiveness. Thus, skilled execution of these concepts—often subtle in nature— requires judicious oversight and continual reference to what a university is as well as what it wants to become. The following example illustrates how significant such subtle changes can be in their impact on a university's spirit.

As dean I threw myself into fundraising with considerable élan. Convincing friends of my university that they needed to invest handsome sums of money to help make it a better institution came easily enough. We had a very good story to tell about how our educational programs added value to people and deeply touched their lives. I merely delved into our alumni to find truly inspiring stories of how graduates transformed their lives and that of their families through higher education. It was fun, not work, to make friends on behalf of my institution.

One week late in the fall semester, I received a colorful invitation from the president inviting me to attend "The Hanging of the Greens." How characteristic of a university in the West, I thought. The Wild West has always been renowned for public lynching as social entertainment. I wondered what dastardly crime the Greens had committed to justify their execution. Cattle rustling? Murder over a card game gone sour? Altercations from a land grab?

Our "Hanging of the Greens" refers, of course, not to a public lynching but a public demonstration of gratitude for the bounty of an ending year and the arrival of a new one. Today religious overtones are carefully massaged so as not to offend anyone, thus slightly diminishing the rituals. Nonetheless, the Hanging of the Greens has always been a longstanding tradition on campus, where students put aside studying for finals, faculty stop their scholarly endeavors, and the community is invited to share a little joy.

The president's house is festively decked out while luminaries— the Southwest's unique candles in brown bags—line sidewalks and buildings across campus. It is truly an impressive and nostalgic sight to see this beautiful scene. Occasionally it is made that much more alluring by a gentle snowfall. Students, faculty, staff, and community members file into the president's house for hot cider, turkey, tidbits, and sweets. Warm conversation moderates the chill waiting outside. Meanwhile, carolers stroll across campus gradually ending up at the president's house to "hang the greens."

I called the president's assistant and indicated that I had decided to bring a ninety-four-year-old widow with me for this joyous occasion. She had been generous in her own way to the school, but that wasn't why I took her along as a guest. As with many of our donors, we had formed a close friendship, and I wanted her to see our university at one of its best moments. Her presence would add to the communal sharing, and she might leave a little better for the experience.

The night arrived cold with clear skies. Two days earlier, a foot of snow had carpeted campus. Much of it had already melted, but you knew what season held reign. I picked my friend up at her house and drove to the president's house. His assistant knew what to do, and to my relief there were two able-bodied students waiting with the president's wife to escort her into the house when I pulled up. Having dropped off my load, I sought parking down the street.

I wish I could adequately convey how pleasant the evening passed. It was one of those most special of moments, a time when our big university in a big city suddenly seemed much smaller and more intimate. It was as though we stepped back forty years on campus. There were no cynical discussions with faculty colleagues. Students were out of their shells conversing freely with strangers. Emeriti faculty littered the crowd. All ages attended. My friend had suddenly found a house full of new acquaintances, and I left her with a multitude of admirers sharing stories to her heart's desire.

About an hour and a half after we arrived, the president announced that the carolers were coming. We ran for our coats, gloves, and scarves and spilled outside. The crowd automatically parted without any directives, sensitive to my friend and her walker. She was gently and gradually ushered to the front so that she would see the carolers as they came up the walk—belting out carols with resonant voices, full of cheer, full of compassion. I scanned the audience and took away an everlasting image of a community sharing love.

Months flew by. In the fullness of time my friend passed away—a loss to our community. Some weeks later, I received an announcement from our *new* president about "The Hanging of the Greens." I indicated that I would attend and went about my business until the following week.

Our new president had embarked on a number of cost-saving measures due to the budget deficit he inherited from his predecessor. All semester long I had been translating those measures into reality at my school. It had not been a fun-filled semester, but that invitation for "The Hanging of the Greens" raised my spirits as I thought back to previous lynchings and the glow of a community sharing in a special way at a special time of year. We may be tightening our belts, but you can always count on a revival of the spirits during "The Hanging of the Greens."

On the appointed night, I walked slowly up the courtyard path to the president's house. A soft golden glow infused the windows with people crowded together as a backdrop. I was greeted politely at the door by the new president and told to go on in and join in the festivities. But they were sadly lacking.

The budget crisis had cut into our ceremony. Gone were the hot cider, turkey, desserts, and luscious tidbits. A few cookies and punch laid waiting on a sorry-looking table. The emeriti had not been invited this year, nor the community. Tight times call for tight measures. Suddenly it was just a bunch of administrators and students with a few faculty members. The bubble had burst, and after taking a cookie, I cleverly extricated myself out a side door and down the walk. Only then did I notice how sparse the luminaries were this year. I went home in a funk.

The moral of this story relates to the unique spirit of a university. We did not balance our resource management with the very soul of our institution. Instead, we let the times destroy something that was highly unique to this campus. The execution of strategy failed the test of respecting our university's spirit.

Does a turkey really cost that much? Had I been given the opportunity or known beforehand that cost-cutting had sliced turkey from the menu, I would have donated a few turkeys. Complimentary food and beverages were more than just a free handout; they represented a communal feast around which we all celebrated being one. "The Hanging of the Greens" had come to represent our close-knit community in which we all shared. Despite forces driving up enrollments and growth in the city it remained a community in which every person was important. It was the essence—the spirit—of our university. Once lost, it has never returned.

Shining Towers of Ivory

The term "ivory tower" has come to connote something derogatory—institutions that are not grounded in reality. Universities are viewed by the public as something just south of unreal. They are enormous money pits into which are thrown good resources that might be better used elsewhere. Those who work in universities are seen as lazy and overpaid. Universities have a nasty reputation for being social employment projects that primarily benefit spoiled professors and incompetent staff who couldn't find jobs in the real world. The public conjures negative images of universities before they think of positive images.

It's time to take back the dingy halls of academe and make them into shining ivory towers—something that everyone can feel proud about regarding how they contribute to society and people's lives. The solutions are so simple. It doesn't take rocket science, just an enormous helping of plain old common sense. Let's scale those walls and sweep in a fresh new perspective while throwing the barbarians out on their collective rear ends in the dust and the muck. Let our institutions of higher education return again in glory as gleaming ivory towers of enlightenment.

REFERENCES AND CITATIONS

CHAPTER 1. PRELUDE TO CONSTRUCTIVE EVOLUTION

P. Altbach (ed.). *American Higher Education in the Twenty-First Century: Social, Political and Economic Challenges.* Baltimore: Johns Hopkins University Press, 1998.

D. Bok. *Our Underachieving Colleges.* Princeton, NJ: Princeton University Press, 2006.

D. Bok. *Universities in the Marketplace: The Commercialization of Higher Education.* Princeton, NJ: Princeton University Press, 2004.

C. Braun. "Tough Economic Times Forcing Florida's Public Universities To Reduce Number of Students It Can Enroll." *Naples News,* June 13, 2008.

S. Fish. *Save the World on Your Own Time.* Oxford: Oxford University Press, 2008.

E. Gould. *The University in a Corporate Culture.* New Haven: Yale University Press, 2003.

C. Kerr. *The Uses of the University.* Cambridge: Harvard Press, 2001.

R. Kimball. *Tenured Radicals, Revised: How Politics Has Corrupted Our Higher Education.* New York: Ivan R. Dee, 1998.

B. Lamb. "Admissions Staff Predicts Decline in Freshman Enrolled." *Whitworthian,* March 18, 2008.

J. Merritt. "MBA Applicants Are MIA." *BusinessWeek online,* April 18, 2005 http://www.businessweek.com/bwdaily/dnflash/apr2005/nf2005047_8428_db016.htm.

Professor X. *This Beats Working for a Living.* Chicago: Manor Books, 1973.

S. Slaughter. *Academic Capitalism: Politics, Policies, and the Entrepreneurial University.* Baltimore: Johns Hopkins University Press, 1999.

T. Sowell. *Inside American Education.* New York: Free Press. 2003.

C.J. Sykes. *Profscam: Professors and the Demise of Higher Education.* New York: St. Martin's Press, 1989.

Chapter 2. Academia: The Last Great Bastion of Resistance to Change

D. Hayes and R. Wynyard. *The McDonalization of Higher Education.* North Carolina: Information Age Publishing, 2006.

D.A. Schon. *Beyond the Stable State.* New York: Norton & Company, 1973.

U.S. Department of Education, National Center for Education Statistics, *The Condition of Education 2003*, NECS 2003-067, Washington, DC: U.S. Government Printing Office, 2003, p. 46.

U.S. Department of Education, National Center for Education Statistics, *The Condition of Education 2002*, NECS 2002-025, Washington, DC: U.S. Government Printing Office, 2002, p. 101.

Chapter 3. Leadership in Strategic Management

A.A. Thompson and A.J. Strickland. *Strategic Management: Cases and Concepts.* New York: Irwin McGraw-Hill. 1999. pp. 3, 135–136.

Chapter 4. Highest and Best Use of Resources

National Association of State Budget Officers, *2003 State Expenditure Report*, Washington, DC: 444 North Capitol Street, NW, Suite 642.

Stanley Fish. "Promises, Promises." *The Daily Report, The Chronicle of Higher Education.* April 30, 2004. http://www.chronicle.com/jobs/news/2004/04/2004043001c.htm.

Chapter 5. Aligning Incentives with Reality

American Association of University Professors. 1915. "Declaration of Principles." http://www.campus-watch.org/article/id/566.

American Association of University Professors. 1940. "Statement of Principles on Academic Freedom and Tenure with 1970 Interpretative Comments." http://www.aaup.org/statements/Redbook/1940stat.htm.

John Brubacher and Willis Rudy. *Higher Education in Transition: A History of American Colleges and Universities.* New Jersey: Transaction Publishers, 1997.

Walter P. Metzger. "Academic Tenure in American: A Historical Essay." In *Faculty Tenure: A Report and Recommendations by the Commission on Academic Tenure in Higher Education.* Commission on Academic Tenure in Higher Education. London: Jossey-Bass. 1973. p. 101.

Michael Scriven. Thinking Allowed Productions. http://www.thinkingallowed.com.

Chapter 7. Cultivating a Strategy Supportive Culture

Ray Stata. 1988. "The Role of the Chief Executive Officer in Articulating the Vision," *Interfaces*, 18(3): 3–9.

Chapter 8. Tough Love for Customers

Mark Edmundson. *Why Read?* New York: Bloomsbury Publishing. 2004.
Eric Hoover. "Undergraduates Study Much Less Than Professors Expect, Survey of Student 'Engagement' Says." *The Chronicle of Higher Education. Today's News.* November 15, 2004.
Gary McWilliams. "Analyzing Customers, Best Buy Decides Not All Are Welcome." *Wall Street Journal.* Vol. CCXLIV. November 8, 2004. p. A1.

INDEX

About the Author

HOWARD L. SMITH is Vice President for University Advancement at Boise State University and former Dean of the College of Business and Economics. From 1994 to 2004, he was dean at the Anderson Schools of Management and School of Public Administration, University of New Mexico. He was also Director of the Program for Creative Enterprise and the Creative Enterprise Endowed Chair. The author of eight books, he has published over 220 articles on topics in health services, organization theory/behavior, and strategic management in journals such as the *Academy of Management Journal, Health Services Research, Health Care Management Review,* and the *New England Journal of Medicine.*

About the Author

HOWARD L. SMITH is Vice President for University Advancement at Boise State University and former Dean of the College of Business and Economics. From 1994 to 2004, he was dean at the Anderson Schools of Management and School of Public Administration, University of New Mexico. He was also Director of the Program for Creative Enterprise and the Creative Enterprise Endowed Chair. The author of eight books, he has published over 220 articles on topics in health services, organization theory/behavior, and strategic management in journals such as the *Academy of Management Journal*, *Health Services Research*, *Health Care Management Review*, and the *New England Journal of Medicine*.